Melissa K. Norris

HARVEST HOUSE PUBLISHERS
EUGENE, OREGON

Cover by Rightly Designed

Cover Image © Pinkyone / Shutterstock

Published in association with the literary agency of WordServe Literary Group, Ltd., www.word serveliterary.com.

Readers are advised to consult with their physicians or other medical practitioner before implementing any of the suggestions contained in this book. This book is not intended to take the place of sound professional medical advice or to treat specific maladies. Links to other sites are provided for information only—they do not constitute endorsements of those other sites. Neither the author nor the publisher assumes any liability for possible adverse consequences as a result of the information contained herein.

All temperatures noted throughout the book are in degrees Fahrenheit.

HAND MADE
Copyright © 2017 Melissa K. Norris
Published by Harvest House Publishers
Eugene, Oregon 97408
www.harvesthousepublishers.com

ISBN 978-0-7369-6967-3 (pbk.)
ISBN 978-0-7369-6968-0 (eBook)

Library of Congress Cataloging-in-Publication Data
Names: Norris, Melissa K., 1981- author.
Title: Hand made : the modern woman's guide to made-from-scratch living / Melissa K. Norris.
Description: Eugene, Oregon : Harvest House Publishers, 2017. | Includes bibliographical references.
Identifiers: LCCN 2017014015 (print) | LCCN 2017031510 (ebook) | ISBN 9780736969680 (ebook) | ISBN 9780736969673 (pbk.)
Subjects: LCSH: Home economics. | Country life. | Home—Religious aspects—Christianity.
Classification: LCC TX147 (ebook) | LCC TX147 .N8248 2017 (print) | DDC 640—dc23
LC record available at https://lccn.loc.gov/2017014015

Printed in the United States of America
23 24 25 26 27/BP-JC/15 14 13 12 11 10

*To my parents,
for teaching me the old ways and
passing down the traditions of past generations.*

*To those who share and
preserve their wisdom for future generations.*

*To my husband,
who lets me know, for better or worse,
how a recipe really tastes.*

*To Julie and Karen,
for opening your friendship, kitchen,
and soap-making skills to me.*

Contents

Come On In 7

1. Bake 9

2. Simmer 57

3. Culture 87

4. Thrive 127

5. Simplify 171

6. Homespun Holidays 193

Recipe Index 247

Notes 253

Come On In

oday's modern world has many things I'm grateful for, but we're also on the cusp of losing something precious. In our drive-through society and "serve it to me ready to go" way of thinking, we further our hurry-up mind-set. We're always in a hurry to do more, but we never seem to reach the place of rest—the respite we're rushing to.

Deep down, we know we're missing something. Our hearts grab onto the promise of a simpler way—a yearning for yesteryear and a reminiscing of a slower-paced time.

In the pages before you, I share the wisdom of people who lived through some of the hardest years the United States ever faced, the Great Depression. But that title is a bit misleading. Like many of our hardships and darkest times, when we reach the other side, with battle scars and healing wounds, we see the snippets of beauty. We discover we learned what is truly important and what we're really capable of. We pare away the unnecessary and the distractions, and we know what is dear to our hearts. Though we'd never have thought it before, we're grateful for the hard times, because without them, we'd never have gained the wisdom.

That is what I'm sharing with you, passed down from my grandparents, my father (whose earliest years and memories are from the Great

Depression), and many other dear friends and family members, that their wisdom may bless you and not be forgotten.

There is something to be gained by creating things by hand beyond just the financial savings and health benefits of cooking and baking real food. It's a kinship with those who have gone before us. A connection with those who passed a special recipe to us, the memories of those we've shared it with, and a promise to those who will share and make it after us. It is my hope that in these pages you will find simplicity, new recipes, and old-fashioned wisdom that still apply to our modern lives.

You'll discover old-fashioned, from-scratch cooking, and recipes so finger-licking good, they'll become your new go-to's. Because I firmly believe food should be enjoyed, that the best recipes don't have to be complicated, and healthy can still taste good!

You'll find a marriage of the old ways and modern methods—recipes and tutorials for growing your own culinary and medicinal herbs and for making homemade soaps and body care items, and strategies for creating a haven in your home amidst our crazily paced lives. The door is flung open, soup is simmering on the stove, a cup of tea is steaming, and the rocking chair with grandma's quilt and I are waiting. Come on in, friend. Come on in.

Chapter 1

Bake

The kitchen was the hub of our small home. Clad in her apron, my mother could usually be found inside the kitchen nook at the end of the trailer where I grew up. Tall evergreens stood sentinel at the end of our yard; large branches fringed the outside of the kitchen window. During windstorms, the low-hanging branches would sweep across the tin roof. The kitchen faced north into the forest, just feet beyond the thin glass windows, and not much light made its way inside.

Due to necessity and want, my mother cooked all our meals from scratch. Breakfast was oatmeal, homemade pancakes, biscuits slathered with homemade jam or gravy, or eggs with toast. The cookie jar never stood empty, and after trudging in from the hour-long bus ride home from school, some type of home-baked goodie always awaited me.

Food is my mother's love language. And she speaks it fluently.

Dinner was a family affair, often including friends or extended family members. By evening, the kitchen windows were slick with condensation, evidence of the food simmering on the stovetop and baking in the oven. And also evidence of the not-so-well-insulated glass and walls. If you've ever lived in an older trailer, you know exactly what I'm talking about.

My father worked long hours as a log truck driver. He left before dawn and didn't get home until right before dinner. The evening meal was often the only time I would get to see him during the week.

He'd enter the house, the sharp scents of pine and cedar hitching a ride in with him. "Hope you've got enough," he'd say. "I invited so-and-so for dinner."

Mom would survey the saucepan and skillet on the stove. "I'll bring out an extra can of beans and the peaches from last year." She'd turn to me. "Better get the extra leaf for the table."

Soon every burner on the little stovetop would have a pot simmering. Mason jars would offer up their bounty from last year's harvest and then wait empty in the sink to be washed. The only dishwasher to be found was a pair of hands.

The table leaf was stored where we could grab it easily. Dad had a habit of bringing people home for dinner, especially without telling my mother in advance. She learned to cook on her toes. This always made for interesting evenings and supper conversation.

One night the guests arrived, and Dad invited them straight into the kitchen while Mom finished preparing the meal. Our living room didn't get nearly the spotlight the kitchen did when company came.

"Tom invited us over for mazzards," one of the guests said.

My head whipped back and forth from Dad to Mom.

"She's the finest mazzard cook you'll run across." Dad's blue eyes twinkled.

Mom kept her gaze trained straight on the fry pan in front of her. Her grip tightened ever so slightly on the spatula.

I caught another look at Dad. I set the plates with precision, my focus never wavering lest I give something away.

Dad and the couple sat down, and I sat down too. The wood of the worn chair was smooth beneath my hands as I tucked them under my legs.

The gentleman glanced toward Mom as she turned the meat.

"We'd never heard of mazzards before, but we figure it might be something related to a Mallard duck."

I bit the inside of my cheek to keep my lips from twitching upward.

Mom's shoulders stiffened.

"That's a right fine guess." Dad couldn't contain his humor any longer, and a big grin split his face. "Truth be told, I was pulling your leg.

There's no such thing as mazzards, but my wife is a fine cook, and you're invited to stay for supper."

I searched the man's face. My fingers curled around the lip of my chair.

Surprise flared in his eyes for a moment. Silence spilled across the empty plates. He glanced at his wife. And then a grin emerged. "You sure had me."

Mom's shoulders relaxed. "You shouldn't tell people that," she said. Her cheeks flushed, and I knew it wasn't from the heat of the stove.

I caught Dad's gaze. He winked at me. The laughter I'd been holding in burst out. Our mirth filled the cramped kitchen. The couple turned into family friends, and rarely did a supper with them go by without some mention of Dad's famous mazzards.

That wasn't the last time he asked someone over for mazzards. When a line works, you roll with it. And Dad was always good with teasing.

That old singlewide 1974 Fleetwood trailer still stands. My parents purchased a house at the end of the road we all still live on, moving out of the trailer when I entered high school. It later housed my husband and me while we saved up to purchase our property and first home. Even though the tiny kitchen is still there, it no longer has the same warm glow and light I remember from my childhood. The original yellow sink is worn down to the metal in spots from the years of dishrags and water.

But I'm reminded that just like the kitchen of my childhood, even when something is small and dark, God's love fills it, stretching it to hold all who need to enter and find shelter and sustenance. No matter how little we have, when we invite Him into the situation, Jesus multiplies what we have to meet our needs. He takes a tiny kitchen and makes it a place of refreshment for those who walk through the door. He multiplies the single frying pan of meat to feed unexpected guests. He takes our exasperation at having to serve more people than we have resources for and fills us with His strength.

If you drive by the road we live on, you'll dismiss that old white metal-sided trailer with barely a glance. Or maybe you'll think how nice the property would look with a proper home. We're quick to overlook the things that aren't polished or up to the normal standards. But Jesus doesn't look at the outside of things. He looks at the heart. Despite the bleakness on the outside, Jesus enters inside, and when His light spills out, it touches the surrounding walls and beckons others into the warmth. Just like a tiny, cramped kitchen with evergreen branches covering the windows.

Lessons in Hospitality

If I were in the middle of preparing supper and my husband waltzed through the door announcing that he'd invited dinner guests who would be here any minute, I don't believe a smile and grace would be my first greeting.

No. My muscles would go into a hyper state and tense together all at the same time. Pulled between trying to tidy up the living room, making sure the bathroom sparkled, coming up with an idea for dessert and more food, and telling him *exactly* how I felt about the situation, I'd look like a dancing chicken. I bet you'd even find a few feathers littering the floor when all was said and done.

While I know my mother wasn't exactly thrilled when my father did this—and he did it on a regular basis—I don't remember ever watching her throw a fit about it. And as a kid, I would not have missed that had it happened.

Our homes reflect who we are. If our first reaction to having someone visit is stress, that's a sure sign something is out of balance. Don't get me wrong—there's nothing wrong with wanting our homes to look nice and tidy. There's also nothing wrong with our houses looking like people live in them. As I write this, there are two stray socks on a chair, crumbs on the counter that need to be wiped up, and we won't even investigate the floor at this point. That's just at first glance in the kitchen.

The out-of-balance part begins in our hearts. If the first thing I'm focused on is the state of my house and what people will think of me when they see it, my pride is shouting. I want my home to be a haven, a place of rest in a frantic world, a place where relationships can be built and where love spills out of the kitchen. And let me tell you, stressing out about the house and becoming irritated about an unexpected guest doesn't create any of the things I want my home to be.

> Martha [overly occupied and too busy] was distracted with much serving; and she came up to Him and said, Lord, is it nothing to You that my sister has left me to serve alone? Tell her then to help me [to lend a hand and do her part along with me]!

> But the Lord replied to her by saying, Martha, Martha, you are anxious and troubled about many things; there is need of only one or but a few things. Mary has chosen the good portion [that which is to her advantage], which shall not be taken away from her (Luke 10:40-42 AMP).

I've always secretly thought old Mary ought to get up and help her poor sister out. Here Martha is trying to feed no fewer than 13 guests who showed up at her door, without the help of any modern conveniences. Doesn't it make you appreciate your vacuum and dishwasher a tad more?

I'm pretty sure no one remembered how clean Martha's home was that day or even what she served, but every single one of those people remembered how he or she felt. After the last bit of bread was sopped up in the oil, the taste of the meal was forgotten. But sitting at Jesus's feet, listening to His teaching, was an experience they could never forget.

This moment of feeding their souls was interrupted, however, by a frustrated and put-out woman. If Martha was anything like me, she'd probably worked herself into a good state of mad in the kitchen. By the time she made her way to the living room, her sandals slapped the floor in a sharp, wordless retort. Her attitude cut through the air like a January wind. "Don't you care that I'm working, pouring out everything I have left, and my sister hasn't even lifted one finger to help?"

Oh, my friends, how many times have I been there? I've brought the whining pity party not only to my family, but straight to Jesus—just like Martha. *Lord, why haven't You helped me out here? Don't You care about all the hours I've put in and how tired I am? Couldn't You give me a break here? It wouldn't take very much—You are, after all, the God of all creation. I'm not asking for a whole kingdom or anything.*

I don't think there's anything wrong with asking why, but it's the heart and attitude that accompany those prayers that matter. *Don't You care?* He sent His son to be nailed on a cross for us. Yes, He cares.

He doesn't want us to be tired or exhausted. Jesus wants us to reach out to Him long before we reach that point.

> Come to me, all you who are weary and burdened, and I will give you rest. Take my yoke upon you and learn from me, for I am gentle and humble in heart, and you will find rest for your souls (Matthew 11:28-29).

Just reading those words eases the muscles in my shoulders.

God has already offered me a break, but I'm too stubborn to see it. (I'm not far off from those stiff-necked Israelites sometimes.) God's grace is our break, and it's available to us every day. So often I clamor for His grace but then neglect to extend it to others.

Hospitality starts in the heart and flows out in our deeds.

There are many nights when I'm in the kitchen cleaning up supper and preparing food for the following day. The clock ticks toward 8:30, and I realize I've hardly sat down since the morning. My day starts at 5:30 a.m. with writing and work on my podcast, blog, and website. Then I get the kids up and off to school, have my morning devotions, exercise, take care of the farm animals and garden, make breakfast, and then drive to my day job.

By the time evening rolls around, my feet ache and I long for the comfort of my recliner. The last thing I want to do is finish making lunches for everyone for the next day. Why am I the only one who makes lunches?

And right there Martha and I become best friends again.

Now for starters, I'm not saying that people in your household and family shouldn't help. I'm not saying you have to be super woman and all of this falls on your shoulders and you'd better be able to bear it, sister. No. Please, don't misunderstand me. If you're truly overwhelmed and believe you don't have any help, I think you should sit down with the members of your family and come up with a plan. Maybe your children aren't so young anymore, and it is time for them to start making lunches or helping with some routine chores. The important part is when you go to speak with them, *you don't do it with a Martha attitude.* Make sure you're approaching them and the situation with grace.

When I'm tired and I still have work to do, I've learned to go to the Lord in prayer. Instead of saying, "I don't know how I can get all of this done, I'm exhausted, and I can't do even one more thing," I remember these words from Scripture:

> I will refresh the weary and satisfy the faint (Jeremiah 31:25).

> Whatever you do, work at it with all your heart, as working for the Lord, not for human masters (Colossians 3:23).

The motive behind the deed is the most important part. When I shift my focus off myself and onto God, reminding myself of His desires, my strength is renewed. This meal I'm making will provide strength and nourishment for the people I love, and preparing it at home saves us money. (Frugality is something that definitely keeps me motivated.) Next, I begin to list all the good things that person does for me. By the time I'm done preparing that meal or whatever task I'm doing, I'm refreshed and ready to go wrap them up in a big hug instead of yelling at them for not helping.

Feed the soul first and there will be enough to fill everything else.

7 Great Depression-Era Tips

1. Quick breads, such as biscuits and corn bread, were very popular and common during rough times. A biscuit had more versatility than a loaf of bread and didn't require the addition of yeast or the longer rise time. You could make biscuits and cover them with white gravy, spread them with butter and droplets of golden honey, slather them in homemade jam, fill them with sandwich makings for lunch or an egg and cheese for breakfast, or eat them plain for a snack.

2. My father recalls my grandmother making her biscuits right in the flour sack. She'd wash her hands, create a well in the middle of the flour in the sack, and mix everything right there.

3. A Great Depression–style pantry consists of whole food items—very basic foods that can be made into a variety of different dishes. Flour (or wheat berries to grind into your own flour) can be used to bread and fry meat; make baked goods, biscuits, and breads; and used as thickener for gravies and sauces.

4. During those hard years, dried beans were a frugal and easy way to stretch a meal. They could be cooked with a bit of bacon or ham bones and served with cornbread or biscuits. Beans simmered with garden vegetables filled many a tummy.

5. Simple foods were served during the Depression years. Bread and lard sandwiches were a common dish, as was a simple meal of freshly baked bread, sliced tomatoes from the garden, and corn on the cob or fresh-picked greens.

6. Potatoes helped fill in the gap for many families. Diced and fried, you could add a jar of stewed tomatoes or other vegetables when there wasn't any meat available, and cook an entire meal in one big skillet.One of our favorite recipes is breakfast potato cakes made from leftover mashed potatoes. I add an egg and a dash of milk with some onion and garlic powder. I shape them into patties, preheat a cast iron skillet with a small amount of oil, and then fry the potato patties. When I pull them out, I grate a little bit of cheese on top. It's a great way to shape your breakfast. You don't even have to use an egg, making it even more frugal.

7. The water you use from boiling your potatoes has starch in it, so save the water to use as a replacement for milk in your bread recipes. This is a big carryover from the Great Depression era, when cows ran dry or there was no money to purchase dairy. You can put the potato water in the fridge for up to a day before using in your recipe. You could freeze it, but it's best used in a recipe immediately. A family friend who is an excellent baker uses only potato water in her cinnamon rolls.

One of the reasons I remember my mother in our kitchen so much growing up is because she was. All our meals were prepared from scratch. We didn't have takeout, drive-throughs, or restaurants. Delis and convenient boxed meals weren't in the budget.

We never went without, but cooking from scratch was a necessity. Knowing there was little money, grocery shopping was done according to what was on sale and what could be stretched the furthest, not by one's desire for a certain dish on a given night. And with three teenage boys in the house during the early part of my parents' marriage, creativity was a must.

I never remember being deprived or feeling like we lived on rice and beans. In fact, my friends loved to have dinner at our house because the food was so good. I still call up Mom and ask for recipes when I recall a dish from my childhood that I don't have written down.

One of the ways she stretched a meal was to find another side dish—especially on the nights when guests showed up unexpectedly. It might have been as simple as a can of corn or a jar of peaches. And of course, some sort of bread item was served at every meal.

In the pages that follow you will find old-fashioned cooking at its finest. There's a reason certain recipes and dishes have been served and passed down for generations. These are the foods I serve my family and my mother served me. They nourish the soul along with the body. May they fill your table, mouth, and hearts...just as they have ours.

* * *

Spelt Flour

Bread is a good filler item, and there's a reason it's been a staple in man's diet for thousands of years. If you're wanting a healthier flour, you may want to go the route I did.

Spelt is an ancient wheat grain mentioned by name in the Bible. It works as a great whole wheat pastry flour. Spelt has a higher protein count and higher water solubility than regular wheat flour, and it also contains all nine amino acids and is much easier to digest. Its gluten content isn't as high as regular all-purpose flour, so when using it in a standard recipe, use 1¼ cups spelt flour for every cup of regular flour as a general guide, or use the same amount of flour but cut the liquid by a quarter: for example, 1 cup of milk would be ¾ cup of milk if using spelt flour.

I grind my own spelt flour, but you can usually find it preground in the health food sections of grocery stores, specialty baking areas, or online.

Chocolate Chip Cookies

Is there any more beloved cookie than chocolate chip? I always bake half of the cookies the day I make this dough and the rest gets formed into a log for the freezer to be transformed into the perfect cookie. This recipe has been adapted from my mom's original recipe because we don't use shortening at our house.

> 1⅓ cups softened butter
> ¾ cup brown sugar
> ¾ cup white sugar
> 2 eggs
> 2 tsp. vanilla
> 3 cups flour, sifted (for chewier flat cookies, use 2½ cups flour)
> 1 tsp. baking soda

1 tsp. salt (if using salted butter, make it closer to ½ teaspoon)

2 cups semi-sweet chocolate chips

Preheat oven to 375°. Cream together the butter and sugars for 3 to 5 minutes. (I've tried using coconut oil, but if you use coconut oil only do 1 cup, as it tends to spread out and make flat cookies.) Mix in the vanilla and eggs. In another bowl, stir together the flour, soda, and salt. Combine the dry ingredients with the wet and stir in the chocolate chips.

Drop by the rounded tablespoonful onto a cookie sheet. (A small ice cream scoop helps keep cookies uniform.) Bake for 8 to 10 minutes, until the cookies are just barely browned on the top, and then remove from the oven. Let the cookies sit on the sheet for 5 minutes before transferring to a cool rack. This helps create soft, melt-in-your-mouth cookies.

Flaky Buttermilk Biscuits

One of the most versatile bread items—and one of the tastiest—is the humble biscuit. This little darling can be ready to go, from start to finish, in 20 minutes. If you've ever had biscuits in the can from the store, once you try this recipe, you'll never want to use store-bought again. This biscuit recipe makes the best, flakiest, melt-in-your-mouth biscuits you'll ever eat. I'm serious—you may well want to double the recipe. This recipe is courtesy of my mother, considered one of the best bakers in our valley, as my older brother proclaims and I concur.

If you don't have buttermilk, do *not* substitute regular milk. Instead, add 1 tablespoon lemon juice to the milk and let sit for a few minutes until it's curdled. You can also learn how to make real buttermilk at home on page 116. As to the flour, you can try a mixture of part whole wheat and all-purpose flour, but you get the most flakiness from straight all-purpose. (Shhh, don't tell my grain mill!)

2 cups all-purpose flour
1½ tsp. baking powder
½ tsp. baking soda
½ tsp. salt
2 tsp. honey
½ cup cold butter, cut into small pieces
¾ to 1 cup buttermilk

Preheat oven to 400°. In a large bowl, mix together the dry ingredients. Using a pastry cutter (or two forks, but you'll be making these enough to get yourself a pastry cutter), cut in the butter until it turns the flour into little pea-sized clumps. Add the honey and buttermilk and stir until just combined. Start with ¾ cup of buttermilk and only add the last ¼ cup if needed to hold the dough together.

Dump the dough out onto a lightly floured surface and fold it together a few times with your hands. Pat out into a 1-inch thick circle. The key to flaky biscuits is to not overhandle the dough. You want the butter to melt as it bakes (this is where the wonderful flaky layers comes from) and not from the heat of our hands by overkneading or overmixing.

This is important: I used to cut out my biscuits with an upside-down glass. Don't do it. If you want a mile-high biscuit (and you do), use a metal biscuit cutter. This cuts through the dough cleanly, allowing it to rise easily. A glass cup actually pinches the sides of the dough closed, making a short, squat biscuit.

Place your biscuits in a cast-iron skillet or on a baking sheet and bake for 15 to 18 minutes, until the tops turn a luscious golden brown.

Biscuit dough freezes really well. I often make a double batch and freeze the second sheet of unbaked biscuits. After an hour or so (or whenever you remember), transfer the biscuits to a sealable freezer container and store in the freezer for up to six months. Take out and bake as normal whenever the urge (or unexpected company) hits you. You may need to increase baking time by 2 minutes.

Crackers

One of the areas I struggle with in my from-scratch journey is snack foods. The packages in the store are so tempting, for both their ease of use and the taste, but the price tag and ingredients make me cringe.

Relax. I've got a cracker recipe for you that not only tastes great, but is quick. The dough whips up in 5 minutes, and the crackers are baked in 10 minutes, meaning homemade crackers are ready for you to eat in just 15 minutes. Can we say faster than a trip to the store?

1¼ cups flour (whole wheat, fresh ground, or all-purpose)

¼ tsp. onion powder

¼ tsp. garlic powder

¼ tsp. chili powder

¼ tsp. smoked paprika (regular paprika works fine, too)

4 T. butter

¼ cup water

1 T. honey

Sea salt to sprinkle on top

Preheat oven to 400°. Measure out dry ingredients into large mixing bowl. Cut in butter until it looks like pea-sized clumps. Add in water and honey and stir until just combined.

Turn out dough onto lightly floured baking sheet or stone and pat into a rough circle. Roll out dough into a ⅛-inch thin circle. (If you don't roll the cracker dough thin enough, the crackers won't be crunchy...but they'll still be delectable.) Use a pizza cutter to cut crackers into desired shapes. Sprinkle with sea salt and bake for 10 minutes. Leave crackers on baking sheet to cool.

Flaky Pie Crust

If you've read my book *The Made-from-Scratch Life*, then you're familiar with this pie crust recipe. It belonged to my great-grandmother and when I tell you it's the best pie crust ever, I'm not kidding. Not only is it melt-in-your-mouth flaky, but it's super easy to work with. I've gotten e-mails and texts the day before Thanksgiving from people telling me they've never had a pie crust recipe turn out before and they're amazed at how easy this one is to prepare, and the taste, oh, the taste—they were talking about it for weeks afterward. No joke.

Our favorite combination of fats is half butter, half lard. Whichever fat you use, it's important that it be very cold (but not frozen, frozen butter doesn't work as well as straight from the fridge). Flaky pastry happens when the fat melts as it's baking, not when you're mixing. If you're using fresh ground flour, chill it before attempting to make the crust. You can also freeze the dough. It thaws well in the fridge and is nicely chilled for rolling out.

This makes 4 individual pie crusts for an 8- or 9- inch pie plate.

> **4 cups all-purpose flour (or 5 cups spelt flour)**
> **1¾ cups cold butter, lard, or coconut oil**
> **1 T. sugar**
> **2 tsp. salt**
> **1 egg, beaten**

1 T. apple cider vinegar
½ cup very cold or ice water

Combine dry ingredients. Cut in butter, lard, or coconut oil. You can even use a mixture of the different fats. Add the egg and liquids, stirring until the dough just holds together. Do not overwork the dough.

Chill for at least 15 minutes.

Divide dough into four equal parts. Turn out onto a lightly floured surface or wax paper. Roll to ⅛-inch thickness. Bake with your favorite pie filling.

To create a baked pie shell for cream pies, roll out one crust and fill an 8- or 9-inch pie plate, fluting up your edges. Pie crusts will puff up if baked without anything in them, so you have two options. First, you can use a fork to prick the sides and bottom of the pie crust (don't worry, the filling covers all that up) fairly generously. Second, you can fill the crust with pie weights. You can either purchase pie weights or line your crust with parchment paper and fill the crust with uncooked dried beans or rice. The liner of parchment paper helps keep the rice or beans from sticking to the dough and makes removal a breeze.

Preheat oven to 475° and bake for 8 to 10 minutes. For hot pies (cooked fillings) use the pie crust when it's hot. For chilled pies, let it cool before filling.

- -

Buttermilk Pie

You can't get much more old-fashioned and simple than a buttermilk pie. Back when almost every home had chickens and a milk cow, the ladies would look for a way to use what they had on hand to fill out their meals. Some buttermilk pie recipes call for lemon, but many homes of old, especially those in colder climates, would not have had easy access to citrus fruits, so I chose not to include it in this recipe.

A buttermilk pie is especially common and traditional to serve during the holidays. For the crust, use the Flaky Pie Crust recipe on page 23 or the Sourdough Pie Crust recipe on page 99. This makes one 9-inch pie.

> **1 unbaked pie crust**
> **3 eggs**
> **½ cup soft butter**
> **¾ cup brown sugar**
> **¾ cup white sugar**
> **3 T. flour**
> **1 cup buttermilk**
> **2 tsp. vanilla**
> **¼ tsp. salt**
> **½ tsp. ground nutmeg**

Preheat oven to 425°. Roll out pie crust and place into a 9-inch pie plate. Crimp the edges and set aside.

Beat eggs in a large bowl until foamy. Beat in butter and sugar with the eggs. Next, stir in flour, buttermilk, vanilla, and salt. Pour into prepared pie plate. Sprinkle the nutmeg evenly over top of the buttermilk pie.

Bake at 425° for 15 minutes. Reduce heat to 350° and finish baking for 10 to 15 more minutes. The top of the pie will turn dark, but it will be a delicious creamy custard inside. Make sure to remove the pie from the oven when a knife inserted one inch from the side comes out clean. The center will be slightly wiggly when you remove it, but it will set up as the pie cools. Overbaking makes custard pies weepy and watery.

Chocolate Meringue Pie

This is *the* chocolate pie recipe—as in dark chocolate, smooth, and hard not to devour by yourself. You may want to bake two: one for you and one for everyone else.

I've adapted this recipe from the classic Better Homes and Garden red-and-white-checkered cookbook. This uses cocoa powder instead of chocolate squares, and I call for quite a bit less sugar than many other recipes. This way the sweetness doesn't detract from the wonderful chocolate flavor.

One of the secrets to a good meringue pie is to put the meringue on hot pie filling. Make your meringue right before the filling so it's ready to go.

Meringue

> 3 egg whites (save the yolks for the pie filling)
> ½ tsp. vanilla
> ¼ tsp. cream of tartar
> 6 T. sugar

In a mixer,[1] beat the egg whites, vanilla, and cream of tartar until soft peaks begin to form. Slowly add in the sugar, a tablespoon at a time, and keep beating until it turns shiny and stiff peaks form.

Chocolate Pie Filling

> 1 cup sugar
> ⅓ cup flour or 3 T. cornstarch
> ¼ tsp. sea salt
> 6 T. cocoa powder
> 2 cups milk
> 3 egg yolks, slightly beaten
> 4 T. butter
> 1 tsp. vanilla
> 1 prebaked pie crust for 9-inch pie

Preheat oven to 350°. In a large saucepan combine sugar, flour or cornstarch, cocoa power, and salt. Mix with milk and cook on medium heat until it begins to simmer with little bubbles; continue to cook, stirring constantly, for 2 minutes. Remove from heat (leave your burner on) and whip in the slightly beaten egg yolks. Return to heat and, stirring constantly, cook for 2 more minutes. Remove from heat (turn off your burner now) and stir in butter and vanilla.

Pour into prebaked pie shell and spread meringue over hot pie filling, making sure the meringue touches the crust. This will help seal it and prevent the meringue from shrinking up during baking.

Bake in preheated oven for 12 to 15 minutes, until the meringue is golden on the peaks. Remove from oven and allow to cool completely before cutting into a little bit of chocolate heaven.

Variation: Instead of making the meringue, simply make the chocolate pie as indicated, pour filling into baked and cooled pie shell, and chill in fridge for 2 hours. Top with the whipped cream topping that follows.

Whipped Cream Topping
    1 cup heavy whipping cream
    ¼ cup powdered sugar
    ½ tsp. vanilla

Place chilled cream in a mixing bowl and whip until stiff. Stir in the sugar and vanilla until dissolved. Spread over top of pie and serve.

To make powdered sugar at home, simply place regular sugar in a high-powered blender or food processor and pulse until powdered. If you pulse too long, it will clump a little bit due to heat, but it will still whip up just fine when added to the cream.

Carrot Cake with Buttermilk Syrup

Of course, carrots make one of the best cakes there is. You can whip up a 9 x 13-inch cake for a crowd in no time with a carrot cake. Most of you are familiar with cream cheese frosting on a carrot cake, but that's only because you've never had it topped correctly before. You'll never miss it now that you have this recipe. Trust me, it makes the best carrot cake you will ever have. You may never go back to cream cheese frosting again.

3 eggs
½ cup melted butter, melted coconut oil,
    or avocado oil
¾ cup buttermilk
1½ cups sugar
2 tsp. vanilla
2 cups flour
2 tsp. baking soda
1 tsp. cinnamon
1 tsp. nutmeg
½ tsp. salt
2 cups grated carrots
1 can (8½ ounces) crushed pineapple, drained
    (If you don't have any crushed pineapple, increase
    grated carrots to 3 cups, add ¼ cup brown sugar,
    and increase oil amount to 1 cup total.)

Preheat oven to 350°.

In a large bowl beat together eggs, oil, buttermilk, sugar, and vanilla. Mix together the dry ingredients and stir into wet ingredients. Then add the carrots and pineapple and mix until combined.

Pour into a greased 9x13 pan and bake for 45 minutes.

When it comes out of the oven, began preparing the Buttermilk Syrup.

Buttermilk Syrup

⅓ cup sugar
⅛ tsp. baking soda
¼ cup buttermilk
¼ cup butter
½ tsp. vanilla extract

Combine the sugar, baking soda, buttermilk, and butter in a small saucepan. Bring to a boil over medium heat and boil for 5 minutes. Stir often and keep a close eye on it—once it boils it will boil over very easily. I turn my heat down to medium low and allow to simmer.

Remove from heat and add ½ teaspoon vanilla extract. Poke holes in top of cake with a toothpick and pour glaze over still-warm cake. Allow cake to soak up the glaze a bit before cutting and serving.

Pumpkin Applesauce Cake

Growing up, I learned to use what we had. Butter and oil can get expensive, but during the height of apple season, you can get second apples (some blemishes and bruises) very cheap, if not often free. While they might not be a crisp eating apple, they make great applesauce.

Mom always made applesauce in the fall. It's truly best warm right off the stove. We love it over biscuits, on pancakes, and of course, just for plain eating. The other reason I love applesauce is because I can use it in my baking as a substitute for oil. This is one of our favorite fall cakes. Pumpkins and apples should play together more often.

4 eggs
1½ cups sugar
¾ cup applesauce
¼ cup melted coconut oil or butter
2 cups cooked pumpkin or 1 can (15 ounces) pumpkin
2 cups flour
2 tsp. baking powder
1 tsp. baking soda
2 tsp. cinnamon
1 tsp. salt

Preheat oven to 350°. In a large bowl, mix the eggs, sugar, applesauce, oil, and pumpkin. Beat by hand until light and fluffy (or use an electric mixer).

In another bowl, mix together the flour, baking powder, baking soda, cinnamon, and salt. Stir into pumpkin mixture until thoroughly combined. Spread evenly in a 9×13 pan. Bake 25 to 30 minutes. Top with Buttermilk Syrup (page 28).

Peach Pudding Cake

If you've never had an old-fashioned pudding cake before, you, my friend, are in for a treat. They don't require any frosting nor do they require making actual pudding or using those little boxes filled with powdered stuff.

A pudding cake is a cross between a cake, pie, and cobbler, but oh-so-simple to make and just about the best thing that will cross your lips all day. This recipe was inspired by my friend Laurie at Common Sense Homesteading.

> 2 cups diced peaches
> Dash of cinnamon (optional)
> Dash of nutmeg (optional)
> 1¼ cups sugar, divided
> 1 tsp. baking powder
> ¼ tsp. salt
> ½ cup milk
> 3 T. melted butter
> 1 tsp. vanilla extract
> 1 cup flour
> ½ cup sugar
> 1 T. cornstarch
> ¾ cup boiling water

Preheat oven to 350°. Scatter peaches in an 8-inch cast iron skillet (a square pan will work too) and sprinkle with a dash of nutmeg and cinnamon if you like.

Mix together ¾ cup of the sugar, baking powder, salt, milk, melted butter, vanilla, and flour. Spread batter over top of fruit.

Stir together the remaining ½ cup sugar and cornstarch in a bowl until combined. Sprinkle over the top of the batter.

Pour the boiling water over the top of the batter and pop in the preheated oven. Bake for 45 minutes or until a toothpick comes out clean. The beauty of this cake is that the boiling water and cornstarch create a thick delectable pudding that melts in your mouth.

Variations: You can use any fruit in this pudding cake, making this a true old-fashioned recipe that lends itself to whatever fruit is in season or you have in the freezer. Use two cups of whatever fruit you choose. Here are some of our family's favorite recipes.

- *Apple:* Thinly slice apples and sprinkle with ½ teaspoon cinnamon.
- *Blackberry:* Sprinkle berries with a dash of cinnamon and nutmeg.
- *Blueberry:* Sprinkle berries with ½ teaspoon cinnamon and 1 teaspoon lemon juice.
- *Cherry:* Sprinkle fruit with ½ teaspoon almond extract and ½ teaspoon vanilla

Great Depression-Era Tip

Rice pudding was a frugal dish for breakfast or dessert. Dried fruits could be added for variety and flavor, but it was often made with the items on hand. Rice can also be used to help a pot of soup or stew stretch further.

Custard Rice Pudding

You'll find many puddings in older cookbooks. It was a way to use up odd and ends of food that weren't enough on their own to feed an entire family, but when transformed into a pudding, could serve a family. Many of these baked pudding dishes made sure food didn't go to waste. As a bonus, they allow you to pop the dish in the oven instead of standing over a stove flipping or cooking items individually.

This first pudding recipe comes from my mother's kitchen. While I did eat it cold growing up, one can only wait so long before diving in, and because baking the pudding seems to take forever when you're little, it's best served warm. Patience and I had a tough time becoming friends when I was little, and we occasionally still squabble.

> **2 eggs**
> **½ cup sugar**
> **¼ tsp. salt**
> **2 cups milk**
> **½ tsp. vanilla**
> **2 cups cooked rice**
> **½ cup raisins or other dried fruit of choice (optional)**
> **Dash of nutmeg**

Preheat oven to 350°. In a mixing bowl beat eggs, sugar, and salt slightly to mix. Add in milk, vanilla, rice, and raisins; stir until well combined. Pour into a 1-quart baking dish. Sprinkle with nutmeg.

Fill a larger pan with water 1 inch deep. Place prepared rice pudding dish inside of the pan of water. Bake for 50 to 60 minutes or until a knife inserted 1 inch from the edge comes out clean. This can be served as dessert or breakfast.

Custard Bread Pudding

This recipe originated from the River House Restaurant, a small restaurant that operated on the banks of the river near our home when I was growing up. They were only open on weekends, but they were well known for their bread pudding, one of the only options on their menu for dessert. It's been slightly altered as the original recipe called for a whole lot of sugar, and as much as I love my sweet tooth, the addition of the raisin bread adds its own sweetness, so we had to nix some of the sugar. Both the restaurant and the sweet couple who ran it are gone now. Good recipes live on, acting as a memory and tying us back to times and people we love.

Bread puddings go way back in the kitchens of old. Many times, cooks used pudding as a way to make stale bread palatable. However, if you use stale bread, it's going to taste stale, so I prefer to not go that route.

One of the ways you can make this recipe versatile is to use whatever bread you happen to have. The restaurant always used raisin bread, which adds to the flavor profile, but you can use any type of bread you like.

> 4 eggs
> 1 cup sugar
> 2 tsp. vanilla
> 1 scant tsp. salt
> 4 cups milk
> 2 cups cubed raisin bread

Preheat oven to 350°. Mix all ingredients, except the bread, with a mixer or blender until smooth. Cover the bottom of a 1½ quart size casserole dish (or a dish that is small enough to fit inside another pan with water) with the cubed raisin bread. Pour the mixture over the bread.

Fill a pan with 1 inch of water. Place the casserole dish inside the pan of water. Bake for 1 hour. Test if custard is done by dipping a knife in water and inserting it into the pudding 1 inch from the edge. If it comes out clean, the custard is done.

Variations:

- If not using raisin bread, add ½ cup raisins and sprinkle the top of the pudding with nutmeg.
- Add ½ cup dried blueberries and 1 teaspoon lemon extract. Sprinkle with a dash of cinnamon and nutmeg.
- Add ½ cup dried cranberries to the bread and add the juice of a fresh-squeezed orange and zest to the rest of the ingredients, cutting back the milk to 3¾ cups to allow for the juice.

Chocolate Custard Bread Pudding

2 cups cubed French bread
½ cup semi-sweet chocolate chips
4 cups milk
4 eggs
1 cup sugar
2 tsp. vanilla
¼ cup melted butter
6 T. cocoa powder

Preheat oven to 350°. Grease the bottom of a 1½ quart casserole dish. Place cubed bread in the bottom and sprinkle with chocolate chips.

In a blender, blend the rest of the ingredients until thoroughly combined and pour over top of the bread cubes and chocolate chips. Place casserole dish in a large pan filled with water. Bake for 55 to 60 minutes or until a knife inserted 1 inch from the edge comes out clean.

Serve warm or cold. A splash of whipping cream on top is splendid.

Pumpkin Custard Bread Pudding

3 eggs
1 cup pumpkin puree
¾ cup sugar
6 T. real maple syrup
2 tsp. vanilla
1 scant tsp. salt
2 tsp. cinnamon
½ tsp. ground nutmeg
½ tsp. ground ginger
3 cups milk
2 cups cubed bread

Preheat oven to 350°. Mix all ingredients except the bread with a mixer or blender until smooth. Cover the bottom of a 1½-quart size casserole dish with bread. Pour the mixture over the bread.

Fill a larger pan with 1 inch of water. Place the casserole dish inside the pan of water. Bake for 1 hour. Test if custard is done by dipping a knife in water and inserting it 1 inch from the edge. If it comes out clean, the custard is done.

Sprinkle the top with a dash of nutmeg and cinnamon for a pop of color. You can serve this by itself or with whipping cream or vanilla ice cream.

Doughnuts

Every evening during the fall and winter months, I helped my dad feed our herd of cattle. During particularly cold spells, we'd have to drive down to the bottom pasture where the watering ponds were. Dad kept a big ax in the back and he'd hack through the ice, sometimes almost a foot thick. One year the cold was so deep, we drove the full-size pickup truck out onto the ice so Dad could chop through the very center of the pond with the ax. He inched the tires off the bank and onto the frozen pond. My ears strained for any pop or crack, fingers curled around the door handle.

Dad exited the truck. The headlights reflected off the dark ice. Ice chunks flew beneath the blade of the ax. Water sloshed and my pulse thudded, my gaze sweeping the ice for any signs of weakening beneath our weight.

After a good-sized drinking hole was cut, Dad backed the truck off the pond. Once on solid ground, I decided the event was much more exciting than scary. *Just wait until Mom hears. We get to do all the exciting stuff with Dad.*

When we got home, I flung open the door of the trailer. Warm air bathed my nose and lungs. A tantalizing scent greeted me. My boots clunked down the hallway floor. There, spread out on the kitchen table was one of the most beautiful sights I could imagine. Homemade doughnuts, still hot from the oil, drizzled with glaze.

Let me tell you, homemade doughnuts are a treat worth writing home about, and definitely worth making, even if you haven't just come in from the ice or feeding cows.

> 2 eggs
> 1 cup sugar
> ¼ cup melted butter
> 1 cup milk
> 4½ cups flour, divided
> 3 tsp. salt
> 3 tsp. baking powder
> 1 tsp. vanilla
> Oil for frying

Slightly beat the eggs in a large mixing bowl. Add sugar and mix. Add the melted butter and mix again. Add the milk and mix.

In another bowl, mix together 3 cups of the flour, salt, and baking powder. Add to wet ingredients and combine. Mix in the vanilla and the additional 1½ cups flour.

Roll out dough on a lightly floured surface to ½-inch thick. Using a doughnut cutter, cut out doughnuts. Save those doughnut holes—we'll use them first to test the oil, plus they're a bite-sized delight.

In a deep saucepan (a Dutch oven works best), heat enough oil so the doughnuts can move freely without touching the bottom of the pan when they are frying. Coconut oil and lard are my favorites. Old-fashioned oil temperature test: Stick the end of a wooden spoon into the oil, if it sputters and bubbles, the oil is ready to cook. The modern and most reliable method is to use a thermometer and heat the oil to 375°. Once you add the doughnuts, the temperature will drop down a bit, putting it at the perfect place to transform the white dough into delicious bites of golden brown.

Drop a few doughnut holes into the hot oil. They should turn golden brown after approximately 2 minutes on each side. With the first batch, place them in the oil and at 2 minutes, check the side facing down into the oil—if it's golden brown, go ahead and flip all of the doughnuts in the saucepan and cook for the same amount of time on the other side. If it's not a golden brown yet, let it cook another minute and check again. Adjust the temperature if the oil is too hot (starts smoking) or takes too long to cook. Fry all the doughnuts and doughnut holes, a few at a time, until all are cooling just enough not to burn your mouth.

Using tongs or a slotted spoon, remove doughnuts from oil to either paper towels (for ease of cleanup) or onto a baking rack and let cool.

Yield: approximately 2 dozen, when rolling back in the scraps and doughnut holes.

Glaze

   ¼ cup butter
   2 cups powdered sugar
   1 tsp. vanilla
   2 T. milk

Melt butter in saucepan over low heat. Remove from the heat and then add powdered sugar, vanilla, and milk. Beat until smooth and drizzle over doughnuts. Don't have powdered sugar? No need to run to the store. Put your regular white sugar or evaporated cane juice in a high-powered blender or food processor and run until sugar is powdered.

Variations:

- For chocolate glaze, add ¼ cup cocoa powder with the powdered sugar.
- For maple flavored glaze, add 1 teaspoon maple extract or substitute ½ cup maple syrup for 1 cup powdered sugar.

Cinnamon Sugar Doughnut Holes

¼ cup butter
⅔ cup sugar
1 T. cinnamon

Melt the butter. Mix together the sugar and cinnamon. Dip doughnut holes in the melted butter, then roll in the sugar mixture. Store doughnuts in an airtight container to keep them fresh—if you have any left over, that is.

French Bread

When it comes to bread, there's little as versatile as a nice crusty loaf of French bread. It's delicious hot out of the oven and slathered with a bit of butter all by its lonesome or served with a hot homemade soup.

The other beauty of a loaf of French bread is the things we can turn it into. From bread puddings to stuffing or just plain, delicious bread crumbs. But first, let us bake French bread.

French bread takes a bit longer to make than other breads due to an increased rise time. This longer rise time actually helps create the texture of the French bread. This recipe is adapted from *Betty Crocker's Picture Cook Book*, published in 1956. If you can find old cookbooks, they offer a wealth of information, entertainment, and delicious from-scratch cooking!

> 1¼ cups warm water (yeast activates at 105° to 115° Fahrenheit)
> 2¼ tsp. active dry yeast
> 1½ tsp. sea salt
> 3 T. softened butter
> 4 cups sifted all-purpose flour (if you don't have a sifter, use a spoon to measure flour into measuring cups and level off)

Egg white glaze
> 1 egg white combined with 2 T. water

Mix yeast and water in a large mixing bowl or the bowl for your stand mixer. Let the mixture stand for about 5 minutes or until foamy. Stir in the rest of the bread ingredients until combined. If using a stand mixer, knead for 8 to 10 minutes with kneading attachment or dough hook. If mixing by hand, lightly flour your countertop and knead dough for 8 to 10 minutes. It should feel smooth and elastic, without sticking to your fingers or the countertop.

Grease a bowl and place dough in it, turning it to bring the bottom side that touched the grease first, upright. Cover with a tea towel and let rise for an hour and a half in a warm area. The top of the fridge or in the oven with the light on work great.

Punch dough down. Lightly flour your countertop and roll dough out into a large rectangle about 15x10 inches. Take the long side of the rectangle and roll it up tightly; place it on a parchment paper-lined cookie sheet. If you don't have any parchment paper or a silicone baking mat, grease the cookie sheet and lightly flour it.

With one hand on each end of the roll, gently roll it back and forth to make the loaf longer and tapered at the ends.

Take a sharp knife and cut slashes along the top of the dough at 2 inch intervals approximately ¼ inch deep. Brush the top of the dough with cold water and let rise for another hour and a half.

Preheat oven to 375°. Brush the top of the doubled loaf with cold water again right before baking and place in preheated oven. Bake for 20 minutes, then remove from oven and brush with the egg white glaze. Bake 25 minutes longer.

Remove from oven and immediately slather it with some butter. Allow to cool. Serve and keep remaining loaf on the counter covered with a tea or flour sack towel.

This bread makes excellent bread pudding and stuffing once it's aged for a day or two on the counter. I've left part of a loaf on the counter for five days and then used it to make our Thanksgiving stuffing. It was the perfect texture.

Yield: 1 large loaf, approximately 16 inches long

Old-Fashioned White Bread

My mother received her great-grandmother's cookbook, a 1938 edition of *Watkins Cook Book*. Tucked among its almost eighty-year-old pages are many wonderful from-scratch recipes and notes. Some of my favorite recipes have instructions saying, "Bake in a moderate oven," with no temperature given. This is some old-fashioned cooking!

One of my favorite bread recipes comes from this cookbook, and I've adapted it below. I've used fresh ground hard white wheat and all-purpose flour with this recipe. Both turn out wonderfully.

Another interesting note is the lengthy triple-rise for this bread. Most modern recipes only use two rises, but I'm finding more traditional and older recipes used three rises. This produces some of the best sandwich bread we've ever had. It holds up nicely without being too soft or scattering lots of crumbs everywhere.

Instead of all-purpose flour, you may also use sifted fresh ground hard white wheat, whole wheat pastry flour, or a mixture of half whole wheat and half all-purpose. This recipe makes two standard-size loaves.

4½ tsp. active dry yeast

2 cups warm milk (you can use warm water, but milk produces a richer bread)

2 tsp. sea salt

2 T. sugar

6 cups sifted all-purpose flour

4 T. soft butter

1 T. melted butter

Dissolve yeast in warm milk with salt and sugar and let sit until foamy, about 5 minutes. Add in flour, 1 cup at a time. Mix in 4 table-spoons soft butter and knead dough by hand on a lightly floured surface for 8 to 10 minutes or in your stand mixer with the dough attachment for 10 minutes or until dough passes the windowpane test. (A test to see if dough has been kneaded long enough is to take a small piece and stretch it. The dough should stretch thin enough you can almost see through it before breaking. This is called the windowpane test.)

Cover with a towel and allow to rise in a warm area for 2 hours, until doubled in size. Punch down and let rise again for 1 hour.

Grease pans well. Lightly flour hands and counter. Divide dough in two and pat one piece into a rectangle on the counter; measure the narrow end of each rectangle to the long side of your loaf pan (this will ensure it fits perfectly into your loaf pan).

Roll it up from the narrow end, take the two ends of the roll and lightly tuck them under the roll and place it in the bread pan. Repeat with the other dough ball.

Melt 1 tablespoon butter and brush the top of both loaves with butter. Allow loaves to rise until doubled in size, about 1 hour.

Preheat oven to 400° and bake for 20 minutes. Then lower the temperature to 350° and bake for 40 minutes until the top is well browned and the sides have started to shrink away from the pan.

Take the bread out of the oven and then remove loaves from the pans. Slather again with butter and place loaves on a wire rack to cool.

Master Bread Dough

About eight years ago, I stood staring at the mile-long list of ingredients in teeny tiny print on the loaves of bread on the grocery store shelf. High-fructose corn syrup, monoglycerides, azodicarbonamide, food coloring, and soy bean oil…just to name a few. I don't even know what half of those things are. We should not have to carry a dictionary with us to know what we're eating. Our food should be simple, with simple ingredients. But the only bread that had normal ingredients in it was more than five dollars a loaf. This wasn't a price I could afford on a weekly basis. My family wasn't ready to give up bread, and I wasn't ready to feed them questionable ingredients. Anyone else have that battle?

After sharing my woes with a friend, she told me her dad had found this new bread recipe that just took five minutes a day, and he'd been baking all their bread for more than two years.

Say what? This mamma could totally carve out five minutes for homemade bread.

The recipe came from the book *Artisan Bread in Five Minutes a Day* by Jeff Hertzberg and Zoe Francois, and it's changed my life. Yes, changed my life. I've used this basic recipe for close to a decade. Not only have I tweaked it to make it even more reliable, but I've also used it as the base for many different recipes, creating a master dough and turning my kitchen into a bakery. Imagine this: one dough, always in your fridge and ready to go for bread, rolls, pretzels, cinnamon rolls, pizza dough, and more. All homemade! You'll never pop a can again.

And the best part? Not only does it take five minutes of active time to whip up the dough, it only uses five ingredients. You'll find my basic recipe is slightly different from the one in the book. A friend started making the dough and mentioned to me she'd added vinegar. I started doing some research on vinegar and acid products in bread dough, and I quickly followed suit. Vinegar acts as a natural preservative and helps the texture of the dough. My great-grandmother used vinegar in her pie crust for the same reason. Acid in baked goods creates a better end product, when used in correct proportion. It's why so many recipes use buttermilk.

A few notes: this bread does only take about five minutes of active time, but when you mix up a batch, you do need about 2 hours of rise time. Plan to be home after an hour or so to keep an eye on the rise of the dough. For the flour, you can use whole wheat, all-purpose, or a mixture. If you're just starting baking and eating whole wheat flour, use 4 cups whole wheat and 2½ cups all-purpose flour.

> **3 cups lukewarm water**
> **1½ T. active dry yeast**
> **1½ T. apple cider vinegar**
> **1½ T. salt (both sea salt and pink Himalayan work fine)**
> **6½ cups flour**

Grab a big bowl, preferably one with a lid. Mix the warm water and yeast together. Allow yeast to activate, about six minutes, until it turns foamy. Stir in vinegar, salt, and 3 cups of flour. Continue adding flour 1 cup at a time until it's all incorporated. This is meant to be a wet dough. It's pretty shaggy in texture, so don't worry if it doesn't feel like regular bread dough you'd be kneading. No kneading here!

Cover dough with a clean tea or kitchen towel and allow it to rise in a warm area. You want the dough to double or triple in size. After the dough has risen, cover it with a breathable lid. I have a large bowl with a lid that latches down on both sides, but I latch only one. Or you may use plastic wrap, but don't seal it tightly on the sides. Airtight is not the goal here. Now pop that baby in your fridge. Wet dough is much easier to handle chilled, and the time in the fridge actually helps develop the dough. Best part—this dough sits in your fridge for up to two weeks, allowing you to bake when you want or need to. Yes, sometimes the need to bake is strong.

Ready to bake? Pull out your bowl of dough. Dust your hands and the countertop with a little bit of flour. Or feel free to use a piece of parchment paper to keep the counter clean and line your bread pan or baking sheet.

Remove approximately a third to half of the dough from the bowl. It will stretch, and you'll have to kind of rip it apart or use a serrated knife to separate it. It will also stick to your hands a bit if they aren't well floured.

Yield: 1 large loaf when using ⅓ to ½ the dough

Rustic Round Loaf

For a rustic round free-form loaf of bread, form the dough into a ball on a piece of parchment paper.

Allow the ball of dough to rise for 40 to 60 minutes on the parchment paper. Don't worry if it doesn't double in size or spread outward. You can also place it in a Dutch oven to encourage it to rise upward instead of out. Taking a sharp knife, dust the top of the ball with flour, and create three slashes across the top of the dough (flouring the knife blade will help it not to stick). This gives the bread a more even rise (as opposed to it cracking where it wants to on top) and gives that true artisan feel.

Preheat your oven to 450°, with a large cast iron skillet or baking stone set on a rack in the middle of the oven to preheat also (you could use a cookie sheet in a pinch, but the stones or cast iron radiate the heat better), and a broiler pan on the lower rack.

When the oven is preheated, carefully (use your oven mitts please) slide out the middle rack and lower the parchment paper with your loaf onto the heated cast iron skillet or stone.

Take a cup of hot water, pour into the broiler pan, and shut that oven door quick. The hot water creates a steamy environment in the oven as the bread bakes, giving you that crunchy outer texture and soft interior. If you prefer a softer crust, omit this step. Bake for 30 to 35 minutes.

Regular Bread-Pan Loaf

Grease a regular bread pan or line it with parchment paper.

Flour or grease your hands and take half of the dough from the bowl. Form the dough into a rectangle, the short side being the approximate length of your bread pan. Roll it up into a log and place into your bread pan. Let it rise for an hour.

Preheat oven to 400°. Bake for 30 minutes or until the top is golden brown. Pull out of the oven and slather the top with some butter. Let cool for at least 30 minutes before slicing.

Cinnamon Raisin Bread

Don't get me wrong, there is nothing as wonderful as a hot-out-of-the-oven cinnamon roll, all that ooey-gooey goodness literally dripping onto your taste buds. And that recipe is coming up soon, but first we must talk about the quicker and less sweet—but equally as yummy—cousin to cinnamon rolls. That would be cinnamon raisin bread, or cranberry orange bread, or blueberry bread. You can make all of these rolled bread delights with your master dough. (And we won't even talk about the exquisite French toast they make.)

½ of master dough

1 cup raisins, divided

1 cup all-purpose flour (or whole wheat, your choice)

3 T. melted butter, cooled slightly

2 T. cinnamon

2 T. brown sugar

2 T. white sugar

1 beaten egg

Softened butter or coconut oil for greasing your bread pan

Take your master dough and knead in ½ cup of the raisins and the flour on a well-floured surface. Roll dough out into a rectangle about the same width as your bread pan and approximately 20 inches long. Smear the melted butter over the surface of the dough. Generously grease a standard sized bread pan—don't be afraid of the fat!

Sprinkle, as evenly as possible, the cinnamon, brown sugar, and white sugar over the dough, followed by the remaining raisins. Roll up the dough and place inside prepared bread pan. Let rise for an hour or until doubled in size.

Preheat oven to 350°. Brush beaten egg over the top of the dough with a pastry brush, and bake for 40 minutes.

Variations: Use dried blueberries, cherries, or cranberries in place of raisins. Add the zest of one orange if desired.

Cheese Bread

I like to use cheddar in this recipe, but use your favorite. Optional add-ins for this bread include minced herbs, diced olives, diced jalapenos, and 2 cloves finely minced garlic.

½ of master dough
¼ to ½ cup all-purpose or whole wheat flour
1¼ cups grated cheese

Take the master dough (you're seeing a pattern here, right?) and knead in another ¼ to ½ cup of flour, or enough flour until you can form a dough ball and roll it out. Roll dough out into a rectangle about the same length as your bread pan and six inches wide. Evenly sprinkle with 1 cup of cheese and add in toppings of your choice, or be a purist and just let that cheese shine through, your choice. Generously grease a standard-sized bread pan.

Roll up the dough and place inside prepared bread pan. Sprinkle reserved ¼ cup cheese on top of bread. Let rise for an hour or until doubled in size. Preheat the oven to 375° and bake for 40 minutes.

Cinnamon Rolls

Made-in-Pan Glaze
½ cup butter
½ cup brown sugar

Bread
½ of the master dough
½ to 1 cup all-purpose flour

Filling
¼ cup melted butter
Cinnamon
½ cup brown sugar
Raisins, chocolate chips, nuts, or other dried fruit
(optional)

Grab an 8-inch cast iron skillet and a 6-inch skillet. (A 9 x 13-inch pan will work too, but cast iron is so versatile and truly does wonderful things for yeast breads.) Place butter and brown sugar in the bottom of the cast iron skillets—about two thirds in the larger skillet and one third in the smaller skillet, but I just eyeball it. Turn your oven to preheat and place skillets inside until butter is melted. Pull the skillets out (remember, the handles are hot!) and set them on top of your stove. Turn off the oven for now.

Liberally dust your counter with flour. Take the master dough and place on top of the flour. Work 1 cup of all-purpose flour into the dough, until you can pat it out into a ¼-inch rectangle.

Slather the top of the dough with melted butter and dust or dump (however heavy- or light-handed you want to be) with cinnamon to preference. Sprinkle brown sugar on top and add your toppings of choice. Roll the dough up like you would a sleeping bag. Slice ½-inch-thick rounds and place evenly, filling-side up, inside the cast iron skillets. You'll get 11 to 12 cinnamon rolls. Let rise in the warm oven for about 25 to 30 minutes, or until the cinnamon rolls are all touching and doubled in size.

Remove rolls and preheat oven to 375°. Bake rolls for 20 to 25 minutes, or until they're golden brown on top.

Have a large plate ready and immediately invert the cinnamon rolls to it when they come out of the oven. Let all that lovely glazy syrup in the bottom of the pan drizzle down over the cinnamon rolls. As soon as you can avoid burning your tongue, dig in!

Variation: Chocolate Cinnamon Rolls. In my husband's opinion, it's not dessert unless it's chocolate. I often make chocolate cinnamon rolls. Add ¼ cup cocoa powder to the pan with other glaze ingredients, and ¼ cup cocoa powder sprinkled with the filling ingredients. You can omit the cinnamon if you wish, but chocolate and cinnamon do go well together. Instead of raisins, sprinkle with semi-sweet chocolate chips.

Soft Pretzels

What other snack can go from sweet to savory in one dip? These treats are a thing of beauty.

½ of master dough
1 cup all-purpose or whole wheat flour

Option 1
5 cups water
¼ cup baking soda
1 egg, beaten

Option 2
1 egg, beaten

Preheat oven to 425°. Line a baking sheet with parchment paper. Flour your countertop and plop the master dough onto it. Lightly knead in 1 cup of flour. Tear or cut off approximately ⅓ cup of dough (I just set a ⅓ cup measuring cup on the counter and eyeball it).

On your floured surface, roll the ball out into a long skinny rope. Roll it a bit skinnier than you think it should be—remember, it's going to rise. It should be about 21 inches long. Once you have your long rope of dough, take both ends and draw them back to the center of the dough, twist once in the middle, and press them down onto the bottom half of the circle creating a classic pretzel shape. Don't worry if they're not perfect—you'll be making these again and again, and soon you'll be an old pro.

We have two options for how we're going to "finish" our pretzels before baking. Option 1 is considered traditional while Option 2 is probably a wee bit less work. Option 2 is a variation I discovered at www.SallysBakingAddiction.com, and I highly recommend you try both to see which you prefer.

Option 1

In a good-size saucepan, whisk together the water and baking soda. Bring it to a boil. Get a large slotted spatula (mine was a tad bit smaller than the pretzel, but it still did the trick) and dip the pretzel into the boiling water for 30 seconds. Lift the pretzel out and let the water drip off.

Place pretzel onto prepared baking sheet. Beat egg and brush on top of pretzels (a pastry brush works great). Coat with coarse salt. The bigger the better in my opinion.

Option 2

Beat egg in a shallow bowl. Coat both sides of the pretzel in the egg wash (just like making French toast) and place on baking sheet. Sprinkle with salt.

Bake for 10 to 12 minutes or until golden on top. If you did Option 2, turn the oven to broil and bake for another 5 minutes to get them nice and brown. I set the timer at 4 minutes because no one wants black-topped pretzels, and the broiler and I have a testy relationship.

Variations:

- *Cinnamon-Sugar Pretzels*: Mix together ¾ cup sugar and 1 tablespoon cinnamon in another bowl. When pretzels come out of the oven, slather them with butter, and then dip the top of the pretzel into the melted butter and roll it around in the sugar cinnamon mixture to get a good coating on top.

- *Honey Mustard Sauce*: Mix ½ cup mustard, ½ cup honey, 2 tablespoons plain yogurt, a dash of salt, and a pinch of pepper. Dip pretzels in to your heart's content.

Pizza Dough

1 cup flour
½ of master dough

Preheat oven to 425°. Knead the flour and master dough together. Roll out dough on a well-floured surface and place on pizza pan or stone, or make a deep-dish pizza with an 8-inch cast iron skillet. Pile high with your choice of toppings—my family's favorites follow—and bake for 15 to 20 minutes, until the cheese is nice and bubbly with bits of gold on top.

No-Rise Pizza Dough

If you're pressed for time and don't have the master dough ready to go, try this quick method for pizza dough. All-purpose flour provides a lighter crust, but you can use whole wheat or a mixture of both.

2¼ tsp. active dry yeast
1 cup warm water
2 cups flour

½ tsp. salt

2 T. olive oil

Dried herbs (about 1 tsp. total)

¼ tsp. garlic and onion powder (optional)

Preheat oven to 425°. Mix together yeast and water in a large bowl and let activate for 5 minutes (it will turn bubbly and foamy). Mix the flour, salt, and olive oil into the dough until combined. Next, add in the dried herbs, and garlic and onion powder if using. Once all ingredients are combined, lightly flour your counter and dump the dough onto it. Knead by hand for about 3 minutes until dough holds together nicely. If dough is too sticky, add a bit more flour until you're able to handle it. It should be fairly smooth and just a little bit tacky, but not shaggy wet. Let the dough rest while you prepare the rest of your toppings.

Tomato Basil Pizza

1 pizza crust

Olive oil

Sliced tomatoes

Diced cooked chicken

Mozzarella cheese

Parmesan cheese (optional)

Fresh basil leaves

Our favorite summer pizza is when the tomatoes are fresh on the vine and basil is growing right next to it in the herb garden.

Preheat oven to 425°.

Smear a light layer of olive oil on the dough and place sliced tomatoes and cooked chicken on top. Place the mozzarella cheese over all of it. You can add a light grating of Parmesan on top for a second cheese option and more flavor, because really, can you have too much cheese on a pizza?

Pop pizza in the oven and bake until golden-brown. For an extra kick, add a light layer of pesto to the dough along with the olive oil.

Easy Pizza Sauce

I never purchase pizza sauce, and neither will you when you see how easy it is to make at home. Simply use one 16-ounce jar of tomato sauce. I actually can all of our tomato sauce, so if you're a fellow canner (or soon to be, because in my book you're either a canner or soon to be one), just grab a pint from your pantry.

> 1 pint (or 16-ounce jar) tomato sauce
> 1 tsp. garlic powder
> 1 tsp. onion powder
> ½ tsp. dried oregano

Empty tomato sauce into a small saucepan. Bring to a boil and then turn to medium heat and allow to boil gently for about 10 minutes to allow sauce to thicken up slightly. Stir in spices. Spread over pizza dough.

Variation: Don't have any tomato sauce? Use a pint or 16-ounce jar of whole, halved, or diced tomatoes. Drain off excess liquid and puree in a blender or food processor, then follow above instructions.

White Sauce Chicken Pizza

Grilled chicken is delicious on this pizza.

> 1 pizza crust
> 8 ounces softened cream cheese
> ¼ cup onion, minced
> 1 clove garlic, minced
> ¼ tsp. dried dill
> ¼ tsp. dried chives

½ cup yogurt or mayonnaise
2 cups cooked chicken meat
1 cup thinly sliced zucchini
Thinly sliced onion to taste
Sliced mushrooms
Mozzarella
Parmesan (optional)

Preheat oven to 425°.

Mix together the cream cheese, minced onion, garlic, dill, chives, and mayonnaise. Smear the white sauce mixture evenly over the dough. Toss the chicken, zucchini, onions, and mushrooms over the white sauce. If you have the type of mozzarella that's soft and in a long log, just slice it and place the slices on top (that's our favorite), but if you've got the kind in a brick, go ahead and grate it. If you have Parmesan, grate a small amount on the very top, like a light dusting of snow. You can really use any cheese you want. Put pizza in the oven and bake until golden-brown, about 15 to 20 minutes.

Fake-It Sausage Pizza

This next pizza is one my mom made growing up. We never had delivery or frozen pizzas, but sometimes Mom would make a big pan of this for a treat. Sausage was expensive, and since we had our own hamburger, Mom would make a "sausage" pizza by using ground hamburger and adding a teaspoon of allspice to the meat when browning. You can use whatever cheese you like, but colby jack and mozzarella work well together on this one.

1 pizza crust
Easy pizza sauce (recipe page 53)
1 lb. hamburger
1 tsp. allspice
Cheese of choice, grated

Onion, diced or thinly sliced
Olives (optional)
Green bell peppers, diced (optional)

Preheat oven to 425°.

Smear the top of the dough with pizza sauce. Layer on toppings, ending with the grated cheese. Bake for 15 to 20 minutes, or until cheese is melted and golden.

Chapter 2

Simmer

Buried deep within all of us is a secret longing. A dream not yet fully unfolded, but formed and tucked into the corners of our minds. It fills the nooks and crannies of our thoughts. When we read or hear about someone accomplishing or doing something close to our dream, it rises up inside of us, pushing to break free from the longing into reality.

We may share our dream with those close to us, or we may clutch it tightly, afraid if we speak of it or shed light on it, the dream will shrink.

Every night before bed, my mother would read to me. We had a strict one-chapter rule—no more and no less, even when our heroine had to dangle over the cliff until we could pick up again the next night.

My favorite book was *Little House in the Big Woods*. Our little trailer would morph into the cabin and I would play under the sheltered branches of our evergreens just like Laura and Mary did under their big oak tree. I loved the way words on a page could string together and come to life. Those words transported me across time and plunked me down with friends. Having a little bit of spunk, I always felt Laura was my kindred spirit, especially when she got into trouble.

After we'd finished the Little House series, we began other books. One of those books was called *A Gold Star for Eric* by Colleen L. Reece. My mom told me that Colleen grew up in Darrington, the neighboring town where my mother had been raised, and she was an author.

"You mean people write books for their job?"

"Yes, she's an author. That's what she does."

The seed tucked down deep into the soil of my heart. "That's what I'm going to be when I grow up," I pronounced. We never know which words will become prophetic in our life.

Years went by. I got married and went to pharmacy technician school and started my job at our local pharmacy. Once a week I attended a local writer's group. The yearning was there, and my dream of being published pushed at me.

I attended conferences, wrote faithfully, and submitted my work to agents and editors. Rejection letters came back. This was back when e-mail was in its infancy and I went through many a book of stamps. Our postmaster commented, "You must be quite the prolific writer."

Yes, prolific I was. Making headway toward my dream of anyone else reading my work, not so much. I had the stack of rejection letters to prove it.

As months slid into years, the dream of becoming a real writer simmered in my heart. I kept writing, stealing time in the evenings after work and after my husband went to bed. After I had my first child, I'd slip in a few sentences during naptime or on my lunch break at work.

Ten years after I'd first started writing for publication, I attended yet another writer's conference, but this time—this time!—a literary agent liked my sample chapters enough to ask for the entire manuscript. I mailed it off to her, all my hopes and dreams from more than a decade tied into that thick envelope and ink on paper.

I didn't fret over checking the mailbox each day like before. It would take longer; she had the entire book to read.

Late August rolled around, when the grasses in the pastures reach tall, holding their heads of seed high with pride toward the setting sun. Golden sunlight bathes the valley and seems to catch on the mountain ridge, holding on for just a few more moments before letting twilight take the stage.

It was in this moment, when the sun was suspended, that I opened our mailbox. There was my self-addressed stamped envelope from the literary agent. Like the sun holding onto daylight right before dusk, I held the envelope for a just a few more moments before opening it.

As I entered our driveway, my tennis shoes slowed on the gravel. The letter crinkled in my hands.

Your writing isn't good enough for publication.

Tears blurred the green of the trees, and hope bolted into the approaching twilight. The words were spelled out before me, in literal black and white. What I'd always feared deep down was true: my writing wasn't good enough. *I wasn't good enough.*

Without words, I fell into my husband's arms and cried. My dreams of being a real writer fled in my tears. As I dried my face he said, "You know, if this is upsetting you so much, maybe you shouldn't do it anymore."

And I agreed. The rollercoaster of hoping and being let down was too much. The dream I'd held onto since I was eight years old sank.

My fingers didn't type a single story for more than two years. I quit our writing group.

But you see, God isn't confined to our feelings. He doesn't work like we'd expect and often, not even when we want Him to. He allows us to see His plan when He knows we're ready, and not a minute before.

Even though I'd turned off the heat on my dream of being a writer, thought the dream was dead and over, God had different plans. In the corner of the living room—the lamplight stretched over my Bible— He chose to show me His plan. Despite the loss of my first pregnancy and the struggle to conceive, two children slumbered peacefully in my home. Both my husband and I had jobs.

God had blessed us, and I knew it. So why did I have this restless feeling deep down in my soul? Why wasn't I content with the gifts I'd been given?

Like that first bubble when water begins to boil, my long-sleeping dream rose. A writer. "God, You gave me this desire to be a writer, but if it's not Your plan for my life, please take it away. Show me what You would have me do, not what I want to do, and let me be content with that."

When we surrender to God, He can do things beyond our current wants or expectations.

I used to think I'd wasted those two years by not writing. *How much farther along I'd be if I'd just kept writing in faith of God's calling.*

There are two things I know to be true. First, if you're walking in God's plan for your life, the devil will fight you. Second, no matter what the enemy tosses at you, if you give it to God, He'll turn it into a blessing.

I no longer see those years I stopped writing as a failure or a setback to where I should be. Instead, I see them as a time God was using to evaporate all the things in me that weren't needed, a refining period.

> These have come so that the proven genuineness of your faith—of greater worth than gold, which perishes even though refined by fire—may result in praise, glory and honor when Jesus Christ is revealed (1 Peter 1:7).

I had tied up my worth and value in my writing. The rejection letter wasn't just about my writing; it went straight to my heart as a rejection of me. I was looking to outside sources to validate me, to reassure me I was enough. When we look to anything other than Jesus to show us we're enough, we'll never measure up.

There are so many things we look to as measuring devices instead of where our eyes should be. We turn to the number on a scale, the amount of money in our bank account, the kind of car we drive, the type of foods we eat, our kids' grades or accomplishments, the cleanliness of our home.

I don't know about you, but the number on the scale never stays where I want it. The money in my bank account doesn't grow fast enough. Though I try to eat healthy, I don't always reach for the healthiest thing in the kitchen and I've been known to still munch away on a candy bar or two...or three. (Hey, the mini ones aren't very big.) My house will look amazing for a day—why can't all the unannounced guests come right then?

No matter what, eventually the things we place value on—those things we're looking at to tell us deep down we're a good person, we're doing something right, and we matter—will fail us. There's only one thing that won't.

> The LORD is my rock, my fortress and my deliverer; my God is my rock, in whom I take refuge, my shield and the horn of my salvation. He is my stronghold, my refuge and my savior—from violent people you save me (2 Samuel 22:2-3).

It took me two years to learn the only way I could be whole was to seek Jesus and His will. Chasing the things of this world and what we want are a sure recipe for heartache.

After praying that prayer and truly giving up my wants, God began opening doors for my writing.

He knew I needed those two years to learn that I was enough simply because His Son had died to save me, and because He loved me. Not because I could string words together or at times my prose was eloquent. You and I, we're enough because He knit us together in our mother's womb, He called us to Him, and He shows us His love anew every morning.

God cares about our heart, and once it's in the right place, He will open the doors. They're usually not the doors I'd pick, and often, they're not even doors I knew existed, but they're always the right ones. Though I confess—sometimes I still require a bit of hindsight to realize this.

I don't always enjoy the simmering period, but it results in the most beautiful of things. It takes longer than I'd like most of the time, but in both our food and our hearts, it's only through this process that we get the desired end result.

> Consider it pure joy, my brothers and sisters, whenever you face trials of many kinds, because you know that the testing of your faith produces perseverance. Let perseverance finish its work so that you may be mature and complete, not lacking anything (James 1:2-4).

Fads come and go, but I've found the things that have stood the test of time are the best. A recipe handed down from generation to generation. Kindness and grace when least expected or deserved. Cookware and methods stretching back to the pioneer days and beyond.

Cast iron is by far my favorite in the kitchen, from my skillets to Dutch ovens and loaf pans. You'll discover why in the words below. And if you're skeptical or haven't had the best of luck with it in the past, keep reading, my friend. It's worth the effort to try again.

Cast Iron

The cast iron skillet and Dutch oven are two of my favorite pieces of cookware. Cast iron is superior in so many ways to today's newer cooking pans. Once heated, cast iron retains its heat, making it a more even cooking surface. I get higher and fluffier rolls when I bake them in a cast iron pan.

Unlike pans treated with questionable nonstick coatings that flake off over time and may release chemicals, cast iron will last a lifetime and can be handed down to the next generation. Plus, the 8-inch cast iron skillet works perfectly for brownies and cornbread, while a 9-inch cast iron skillet works great for pies and even deep-dish pizzas. Having fewer dishes in my cupboards is a plus. I especially love that I can take my cast iron from the stovetop to the oven to the wood stove, and even use it outside over an open fire to cook our food.

Don't believe the fallacy that food sticks to cast iron either. If properly seasoned, it becomes nonstick, turning out perfect eggs over easy and pancakes like a pro. It takes very little to care for cast iron, but it is a tad different than regular dishes and cookware. Here's how to keep your cast iron in good condition and lasting for a lifetime.

Seasoning: After purchasing a new pan or one at a garage sale that needs to be reseasoned, wash it out with hot water and a rag. Use coarse salt to scrub off cooked-on food. If it's in really bad shape, you may need to use steel wool to scrub it clean.

Slather it with a thin layer of oil (coconut and avocado work well), both inside and out, then stick it in a preheated 400° to 500° oven for an hour. As the oil cooks, it fills the pores of the pan, forming a nice black finish (this is where stick-free comes in). Don't be alarmed if it smokes—just turn on your exhaust fan.

Even if a pan says *preseasoned*, I still season it myself before use—usually twice, especially if it's rusty or was in rough shape when I got it. The older cast iron pans do have a smoother surface due to the casts. Newer casts are a bit bumpier, but you can still achieve a good seasoning on them and make them nonstick. If you happen to be fortunate enough to run across some old cast iron at a thrift store or garage sale, grab those treasures and give them a fresh seasoning and new life in your kitchen.

Cooking: When cooking eggs or pancakes, make sure to melt butter or oil in the pan first. This will help you achieve a nonstick cooking surface and further season your pan.

Cleaning: Let your pan cool down slowly. Never pour cold water into a hot pan, or it could crack. Never use soap to clean your cast iron. It sounds counterintuitive, but soap will destroy your seasoning and cause your pan to rust. But don't worry—the heat in the pan will kill any bacteria. When your pan is ready for cleaning, just rinse it with hot water and wipe it out with a nonabrasive cloth. You don't want to scratch that seasoning off! If you have baked-on food, scrub off the sticky parts with table salt. You can also find specialized chain mail scrubbers for cast iron pans. Wipe the pan dry and recoat it with a thin layer of oil before storing.

Storage: Your cast iron pans will store best in the open. If you must stack them, always store Dutch ovens with the lid slightly ajar to allow airflow.

Dutch Oven Recipes

Everyone should have a few good comfort food recipes, and that includes soups. Soups and stews can be cooked in a Dutch oven (you saw that coming, right?), and they also stretch the budget to feed more mouths. You can make a complete meal out of a few vegetables and a small amount of meat.

Let's get our soup on!

Chicken Stock

This stock can easily be done with turkey, beef, or pork as well. Save the bones from a roast or whole bird. Don't worry if there's a bit of meat still on there, it just adds to the flavor.

When trimming off the ends of carrots, celery, onions (save the skins too), squash, or any other vegetable, toss them in a freezer container. You'll be surprised how quickly you'll get a few cups from the parts you'd normally discard. You can also use any wilting or needs-to-be-used-up-fast veggies from the fridge.

Place your vegetable odds and ends, about four to six cloves of smashed garlic (again, leave the skins on—less work for you and more nutrition for the stock), and bones in a large stock pot or slow cooker. Pour ¼ cup apple cider vinegar over the bones and let sit for about 15 to 20 minutes. The vinegar will help break down the bones faster and pull out all of the good gelatin and collagen.

Cover with water until all the vegetables and bones are submerged. Toss in whatever herbs you have. Rosemary is a favorite of mine to add in, as well as oregano, thyme, and bit of sage.

Let simmer on low for at least 12 hours. Pour contents (careful, it's hot) through a strainer. I use a fine-mesh strainer or a colander lined with cheesecloth. Place in the fridge or freezer.

Great Depression-Era Tip

Cooking a whole bird, ham, or roast with the bone was a way to make more meals from one item. The bones and skin were saved to make bone broth or soup the following day.

Chili

There are all kinds of theories when it comes to chili, and many swear true chili doesn't include beans—just the meat, peppers, and spices. Staunch supporters of a no-bean chili won't be happy with my version. For many homes, beans are a frugal way to stretch a meal even further. Use any beans you'd like for this chili—pinto, black, white, or whatever you have on hand. Soak your beans for at least 12 hours, but no more than 24 hours, in cold water.

Some people like to use a tablespoon of vinegar in the water when soaking, but I find it causes the beans to be tough. The thought is the acid in the vinegar helps break down and reduce the phytic acid in the beans. However, we noticed the beans didn't seem to ever get all the way done (aka, tough!), so we still soak our beans for 24 hours (which helps reduce the phytic acid) but don't use vinegar any longer.

Drain and rinse the beans thoroughly in clean water.

1 lb. ground beef (or meat of choice)
3 cups soaked beans
3 to 4 cups water
1 onion, diced
5 cloves garlic, diced
1 to 2 jalapenos, to taste
1 red bell pepper
1 qt. drained stewed tomatoes *or* **2 cups tomato sauce**
1 T. honey
3 to 4 T. chili seasoning mix (page 149)

Place the soaked beans in a slow cooker and cover by an inch with water. Add the meat, onion, garlic, peppers, and tomatoes. Cook on low for 6 to 8 hours. If needed, add more water. Right before serving, add the honey and seasonings. Start with 3 tablespoons seasoning and taste. I've found with herbs and seasonings, the flavors are diluted when cooked for a long time, so you'll save on the amount of spices and herbs needed while getting the most flavor by adding right before serving. Add more if needed. Serve with fry bread (recipe follows).

Yield: 8 servings

Fry Bread

This is my favorite dish to serve with chili. Many accounts credit Native Americans with inventing fry bread. It became a common dish in the latter part of the 1800s, when they were forced to depend on government staples instead of their historical foraging, hunting, and gathering way of life and diet. The government gave out flour and lard for provisions, and the humble fry bread was born.

Unfortunately, deep frying foods has gotten a bad rap, and many people shy away from preparing meals this way. Though cooking food in hot oil does add some calories, we consider these meals a treat and not a regular occurrence at our table. I'm more concerned with the type of oil being used. I prefer to use unrefined coconut oil mixed with lard for our deep frying. The mixture of the two together works well for me in keeping a delicate flavor for breads.

I've tried several different versions, and my two favorites are presented here. The first version uses both flour and cornmeal and is great for making tacos. The second version uses all flour and is delicious for making tacos, but it really shines when you prepare it as dessert.

For fry bread, start by measuring out about half a cup of coconut oil and half a cup of lard. Use an 8-inch cast iron skillet, if you have one. Melt the oil over medium-low heat. Once it's melted, you should have about an inch of oil in your pan. After two minutes, check the oil with a wooden spoon. If a little bubble forms around the stick, the oil is ready to use. If not, heat it for another couple of minutes and check again, adjusting the heat if needed. Add your dough of choice from the recipes below!

Remember to keep a watch on your oil, especially if it reaches the smoking point. And if you have an oil fire, never, ever try to put it out with water—this will just cause the fire to spread. An oil fire should be put out by smothering or using a fire extinguisher.

Fry Bread with Cornmeal

2 cups flour
1 cup cornmeal
2 heaping tsp. baking powder
½ tsp. salt
1 cup water
coconut oil or lard for frying (approximately 1 cup)

Mix dry ingredients together. Add water and stir *just* until it comes together; don't over stir or knead it. If needed, add a few more tablespoons of water. Let sit for at least 30 minutes, but you can let it go longer and it won't hurt it a bit. I once forgot it for more than 5 hours, and it then became dinner instead of lunch. Don't you just love a dough that works with you like that?

Heat the oil. When oil is ready to fry, separate the dough into 6 balls. Flatten dough on a lightly floured counter and, using your fingers, push, pull, and mold it into a lumpy circle. I love this, because it looks old-fashioned and doesn't matter if I get it to a perfect thinness. Hear that, pie crust and tortillas? *Rustic* is the new home baker's best friend.

Being careful of grease splatters, add your dough to the oil. It should bubble when the dough hits the oil. Allow to fry for about 1 minute, until it starts to turn golden brown. Flip and finish cooking for 1 minute longer. If your dough isn't browning in the minute time frame, increase the heat slightly.

Place on a plate with an absorbent towel and continue adding layers of freshly cooked fry bread.

Yield: 8

Dessert Fry Bread

3 cups flour
2 heaping tsp. baking powder

½ tsp. sea salt
¾ cup buttermilk
½ cup water
Coconut oil or lard for frying (approximately 1 cup)

Mix dry ingredients together. Add in buttermilk and stir until just combined. Add water if needed. Let sit for up to 6 hours, but at least 30 minutes. Form into 6 balls of dough. On a lightly floured surface, flatten the dough ball with the palm of your hand. Form into a rustic circle. Fry in hot oil for about 1 minute each side until golden brown. Dry on a plate lined with an absorbent towel.

- Sprinkle with cinnamon, a touch of sugar if you want, and drizzle liberally with honey.

- Brush with butter when it first comes out of the oil, and then roll in a shallow dish of mixed cinnamon and sugar.

- Smear your favorite jam or jelly on top, and then dust with powdered sugar or whipped cream.

Yield: 6

Ham and Broccoli Chowder

2 T. butter
½ cup onion, minced
3 cloves garlic, minced
3 T. flour
2 cups chicken broth (you may use water or some
    bouillon, but the flavor is in the broth)
1 to 2 cups milk
1 cup grated cheese
2 cups chopped broccoli (fresh or frozen)
2 cups diced, cooked ham

½ tsp. salt (or to taste, depending upon your ham)
Dash of pepper

Place a soup pot or Dutch oven on the stove and turn to medium heat. Melt the butter, and then add the onions and garlic. Sauté for about 3 minutes or until onions are translucent. Stir in flour until it creates a thick paste.

Pour in 2 cups broth, stirring until fully combined. Add the broccoli and let simmer for about 5 minutes, or until broccoli is cooked, stirring often.

Stir in 1 cup of milk and 1 cup of grated cheese. You can alter the flavor by using your favorite cheese. We really like fresh grated Romano and cheddar together, but Gouda, Swiss, and mozzarella will also taste fantastic! And if you add in some smoked cheese, oh my, invite me over for dinner, okay?

Add ham, salt, and pepper. Let simmer on low, stirring occasionally, for 15 minutes. If it becomes too thick, simply thin with a little bit of extra milk.

For a dairy- and gluten-free option, use coconut oil in place of butter, extra chicken broth in place of milk, and organic cornstarch or arrowroot as your thickener.

Yield: 8 to 10 servings

Son of a Gun Stew

The stew recipe below was named when it was first tasted and someone exclaimed, "Son of a gun, this stew is good." It has been called such ever since. Whenever we lost power, my mother would prepare this on top of our woodstove. It's long been a family favorite. You may use fresh, frozen, or canned vegetables. I use home-grown and canned pints of most of the vegetables, but however you roll is fine.

The secret ingredient is the chili powder. There's not enough to make the stew spicy—just enough to give it the perfect flavor.

1 lb. stew meat
1 T. butter
1 cup onion, minced
2 to 3 cloves garlic, minced
1 cup carrots, diced
¼ to ½ cup celery (optional)
2 to 3 medium sized potatoes, cubed
2 cups corn or green beans
2 cups peas
2 cups tomato sauce
2 cups water or broth
½ tsp. chili powder
Salt and pepper to taste

In a large pot over medium heat, melt the butter; brown the stew meat, onions, garlic, and celery (if using celery). When meat is browned and vegetables are partially cooked, add in the remaining ingredients. Allow to simmer on low for an hour or two, until the potatoes are cooked all the way through.

Serve with biscuits or bread slathered with butter.

Yield: 12 servings

Crab Bisque

I'm going to confess, I'm not much of a seafood lover, but this soup has made me a convert. My husband is happiest out on the ocean, and our summers are planned around the opening of crabbing season. This is his recipe and creation.

5 T. butter, divided
½ cup onion, minced
½ cup carrots, diced
½ cup cooking sherry or wine

3 cloves garlic, minced (about a tablespoon)
¼ cup flour
2 to 3 cups chicken stock
1 cup heavy cream
1 to 2 cups cooked crab meat
1 T. lemon juice
1 tsp. Worcestershire sauce
Salt and pepper to taste
Dash of Sriracha (optional)

In a large stock pot or Dutch oven, melt 1 tablespoon of the butter over medium heat and add in onions, carrots, sherry, and garlic. Sauté 3 to 4 minutes, until vegetables are turning soft. Dump this onto a plate or small bowl and return pot to the heat.

Melt remaining butter over medium heat. Stir in flour until it creates a thick paste. Slowly whisk in chicken broth and allow to simmer until thick, about 3 to 4 minutes, stirring constantly.

Dump in precooked onions, carrots, and garlic. Allow to simmer for 15 to 20 minutes. Use an immersion blender to puree the vegetables into the roux.

Stir in the cream, crab meat, lemon juice, Worcestershire sauce, salt, and pepper. Cook for another 5 minutes, until everything is heated through. If you're like my husband and like some heat, add a dash or two of Sriracha to your bowl only, just to be nice to those of us who don't have stomachs or taste buds made of iron.

Yield: 6 servings

Spaghetti and Meatballs

A homemade marinara sauce is something of beauty, mainly due to its simplicity, giving a true delight to the taste buds. This is an easy way to stretch a few ingredients into a full meal if needed. You can serve the sauce plain over rice or pasta.

I use a quart of home-grown and canned paste tomatoes for better flavor and less water. If you're using dried herbs instead of fresh, decrease the amounts of basil or oregano to teaspoons.

Spaghetti Sauce

¼ cup olive oil
½ cup onion, minced
3 cloves garlic, minced
4 cups stewed or canned tomatoes
¼ to ½ tsp. salt
¼ tsp. ground black pepper
2 to 3 tablespoons finely chopped fresh basil or
   oregano

In a saucepan over medium heat, heat the olive oil and sauté the onion and garlic until tender. Add the tomatoes, salt, and pepper. Either smash tomatoes with a potato masher or use an immersion blender. The potato masher gives a chunkier sauce, whereas the immersion blender gives a smoother texture. Stir in herbs and simmer on low for 30 minutes to an hour, until sauce has thickened.

Yield: 2 to 3 cups

Meatballs

The beauty of meatballs is they are so incredibly versatile. Really, any ground meat will make a meatball—you can use beef, sausage, turkey, ground venison, or a mixture.

One of the bases of meatballs besides the meat is breadcrumbs. Of course, the store shelves have those little cylinder cardboard cans or boxes of breadcrumbs, but they come at a pretty penny when you can easily make them at home yourself. See the next recipe for my method.

1 egg, beaten
¼ cup water or milk
1 cup bread crumbs
¼ cup onion, minced

3 cloves garlic, minced
½ tsp. dried oregano
½ tsp. dried sage
½ tsp. dried basil
½ tsp. salt
Dash of ground black pepper
1 lb. hamburger

Preheat oven to 375°. In a large mixing bowl, beat the egg with a fork until foamy and then incorporate the water or milk. Add the bread crumbs, onions, garlic, herbs (optional), and salt and pepper and stir until thoroughly mixed. Lastly, stir in the hamburger until everything is combined.

With a tablespoon, scoop up a heaping spoonful and roll into a ball; repeat until all of the mixture is made into meatballs. Place them in a 9 x 13-inch baking dish. Bake for 25 minutes.

Remove meatballs from oven. Add to pot of spaghetti sauce and serve.

Variation: Instead of serving these meatballs with spaghetti, spoon or brush on barbecue sauce or your favorite spicy jelly or jam. Return to oven for 3 to 5 minutes (be careful to watch so your glaze doesn't burn). Remove from oven and serve.

Yield: approximately 25 meatballs

Bread Crumbs

Women in an old-fashioned kitchen and home used up every bit of what they had. They didn't run to the store for this and that. Instead, they figured out how to use everything in their home and off their land without letting food go to waste.

One of those things is something the average American doesn't think twice about tossing out: the heels of the bread loaf. But now that I'm about to share how easy it is to make bread crumbs, you'll be like a pioneer cook of old and will never toss those again because you'll be turning them into something fabulous.

The best thing about homemade bread crumbs is the flavor. They add much more depth to the recipe than store-bought ones. Think of mixing together sourdough, whole wheat for nuttiness, French bread, regular white, and any of your other favorites.

There are two ways to dry your bread—because we need it really dry in order to make the crumbs. But remember, we don't want stale, as in really old bread, as that flavor does transfer into the crumbs.

The first is as old-fashioned as it gets: leave the bread out on the counter unsealed (you could lay a tea towel or breathable towel over it) for a couple of days. The second option is to break up the bread into small chunks and put them on a rimmed baking sheet. Bake in a 300-degree oven for 15 minutes, flipping the pieces over halfway through, until they're dried out. Remove from the oven and allow them to cool.

Once you have your dry bread, you'll need either a blender or a food processor. I prefer my food processor for this one. Blend the bread until if forms into crumbs. The longer you blend it, the finer the crumbs. You can also add dried herbs to make savory breadcrumbs.

Use immediately in your recipe of choice and store remaining bread crumbs in the freezer for future use. I pour mine into a quart-sized mason jar for freezer storage. This allows me to know at a glance exactly how many cups I have left for a recipe.

Great Depression-Era Tip

Many foods were prepared with the thought of how they could be turned into another meal. Served fresh, bread is a great addition to supper, but then you're able to take the ends of the loaf and create bread crumbs or bread pudding that takes the food into a second meal.

Barbecue Sauce

If you don't want to use a ketchup base for this sauce, you can use tomato paste and dilute it with water, or boil down stewed tomatoes and add a splash of vinegar and mustard.

> **2 cups ketchup**
> **1 cup brown sugar**
> **½ cup onion, finely minced**
> **5 cloves garlic, minced**
> **¼ cup apple cider vinegar**
> **3 T. Worcestershire sauce**
> **½ tsp. ground black pepper**

Combine all ingredients in a saucepan and bring to a boil. Stir and reduce to a simmer. Allow to simmer for an hour, until sauce has thickened and turned a pretty dark red. Use immediately, or store in the fridge or freezer.

Variations:
- Want a little heat? Add ¼ teaspoon of red pepper flakes or cayenne pepper.

- Add a fruit flavor. For glazes on meat, try a cup of your favorite jam or jelly in place of the brown sugar. Grape, apple, peach, and plum are all favorites at our house. Cut back the ketchup to one cup and reduce the cooking time to about 20 minutes.

Chicken Dumplings

There is nothing more comforting than a big bowl of homemade chicken dumplings. Not only is this old-timey dish a comfort food, but it's actually packed with nourishing things to feed your body during those cold winter months.

One of the beautiful things about cooking from scratch is the ability to adapt a recipe to what you happen to have on hand and the time you have available. If you have an afternoon at home and a whole chicken, then you'll want to take this route. But hey, we don't always have the luxury of a few hours, so I've included variations at the end of the recipe when you need to whip this up quick style, because we should still be able to create wonderful home-cooked meals when we're pressed for time.

If you don't have a whole chicken for this dish, you can also use cuts of chicken with the bone in, about 4 pounds' worth. The garlic isn't traditional in this dish, but it adds wonderful flavor. The herbs are also optional, and you can use any combination you'd like—all of them, if you're feeling daring!

Chicken Mixture

1 whole chicken (or small turkey)
    seasoned with salt and pepper
1 large onion, diced
2 celery stalks, diced
4 cloves garlic, minced (optional)
4 medium carrots, diced
1 bay leaf (optional)
¼ cup fresh thyme (optional)
4 fresh sage leaves (optional)
¼ cup fresh chopped rosemary (optional)
½ cup cream (optional)

Dumplings

1 cup flour
2 tsp. baking powder
½ tsp. salt
½ cup buttermilk (regular milk works if needed)
2 T. melted butter or coconut oil

Place a whole chicken seasoned with salt and pepper in a large cast iron Dutch oven (or a large stock pot if that's what you have) and fill it with water until the water is about ¾ of the way up the chicken. Bring to a boil and allow to gently simmer with the lid on for about 1 hour. After an hour, add the vegetables and cook for another 30 minutes, or until all vegetables are tender. After vegetables are done, using tongs or a big slotted spoon, remove chicken from the pot onto a big plate or platter to cool. Once cool enough to handle, shred chicken and return to pot. Keep remaining carcass to make a batch of homemade broth (I toss mine in the freezer if I'm not going to make broth right away).

To make this really rich and decadent, add ½ cup of cream.

For the dumplings—my absolute favorite part—measure and mix together dry ingredients. Pour in melted butter and milk and mix until just combined. Don't overmix—it will be a bit wet and sticky dough. Drop by the tablespoonful (I just use my mixing spoon) into the stock. Keep chicken stock at a simmer and cook for 10 minutes with the lid on; remove the lid and simmer for 10 minutes more.

For a more traditional dumpling, flour a countertop and roll the dough out to ¼-inch thick. Using a pizza cutter or sharp knife, cut the dough into 1-inch strips and then into 2-inch-long pieces. Drop into chicken stock that is just at a simmer and cook for 10 minutes with the lid on, and then 10 minutes more with the lid off.

Variations:

- *30-Minute Chicken and Dumplings:* Need to make this fast? Use 4 cups (1 quart) of chicken broth, 2 to 3 cups of shredded or diced cooked chicken, and 2 tablespoons butter. Dice fresh vegetables very small, or use frozen or canned vegetables (drained) instead to speed up cooking time. Follow instructions for dumplings.

- *Chicken and Biscuit Bake:* Don't like dumplings? (I'll pretend I didn't know that about you; my mother is the same way.) You can do an oven variation and top this with biscuits. You'll need to prepare it in a cast iron Dutch oven so you can transfer it to the oven, or you can pour the mixture into a 9 x 13-inch baking pan, but be very careful as it's hot! Using the biscuit recipe on page 20, place biscuits on the surface of the chicken soup. Place in a preheated 350° oven, uncovered, and bake for 30 minutes or until biscuits are golden on top.

Shepherd's Pie

Whenever my mother made Shepherd's Pie, I was ready for seconds before I'd even taken the first bite. After we phased out store-bought condensed soups, I had to come up with a version that was still delicious and fit the bill for my beloved casserole.

This is my childhood favorite from the 1980 *Better Homes and Gardens All-Time Favorite Hamburger Recipes*...revamped real-food style.

   1 lb. hamburger
   ½ cup onion, diced
   3 cloves garlic, minced
   1 jar (16 ounces) tomato sauce or 2 cups home-canned
      tomato sauce
   16 ounces canned green beans or canned corn,
      drained
   ¾ tsp. sea salt
   Dash of fresh ground pepper
   2 to 3 cups mashed potatoes
   1 beaten egg
   ½ to ¾ cup shredded cheddar cheese

Preheat oven to 350°. In a large skillet, brown the hamburger, onion, and garlic. Drain off fat. Place this in a 1½ quart casserole dish. Stir in tomato sauce, green beans, salt, and pepper.

Beat an egg and blend in with mashed potatoes. If needed, add a small amount of milk to create creamy potatoes, but not runny.

Spread, or drop by the spoonful, the mashed potatoes on top of the meat mixture. Sprinkle cheese on top. Bake for 25 to 30 minutes, until cheese is melted and everything is hot.

Yield: 4 to 6 servings

Berry Dumplings

I have yet to find the berry that isn't delicious in this dish. Our two favorites are blueberry and blackberry, but experiment with whatever combination of fruits you have on hand.

Berry Mixture

4 cups fresh or frozen berries
1⅔ cups water
¾ cup sugar
½ tsp. cinnamon
2 tsp. lemon extract or 1 tsp. bottled lemon juice

Dough

1 cup flour
1½ tsp. baking powder
1 T. sugar
⅛ tsp. salt
½ cup softened butter or coconut oil
¼ cup milk

Place berries, water, sugar, cinnamon, and lemon juice in a large pot and stir until sugar is dissolved. Bring to a boil over medium-high heat, stirring often.

Mix together all the dry ingredients for the dough, and then cut in the softened butter or coconut oil with a pastry cutter. Add in the milk until just combined into a slightly wet dough.

Drop the dough by the spoonful onto the top of the boiling berries, until most of the surface of the berries is covered. Cover the pot with a tight-fighting lid, turn the heat down to medium-low, and allow to simmer with the lid on for a full 20 minutes (no peeking). After 20 minutes remove lid and serve.

While this would be wonderful with whipped cream of vanilla ice cream, we usually just eat ours as-is. If you happen to have any leftovers, simply heat it back up before serving again. There's just something about warm berries that's the best.

Old-Fashioned Oatmeal

Having been raised through the end of the Great Depression, my father knows a thing or two about lean times. I love hearing his stories and the way it has shaped his thinking and practices. Tough times give us a new appreciation for the simple things around us. Hard times create a thankfulness for what we have, instead of a pining for what we don't.

My father likes his food like he likes his life—simple. One thing I've always been a bit astounded by is his breakfast. Every morning since I can remember and up until today, he has a bowl of oatmeal for breakfast.

If my mom fixes pancakes, waffles, biscuits and gravy, eggs and bacon, it doesn't matter—he still has a small bowl of oatmeal with it. If she doesn't fix anything else, he still makes his pot of oatmeal. And he's quite content and happy with just his pot of oatmeal. I prefer a little more variety in my breakfast. While I'd like to think I'd be happy with oatmeal every morning, I'd probably complain a bit after the first week.

Great Depression-Era Tip

Oatmeal was a filling and frugal way to fill bellies. It can be cooked all by its lonesome for breakfast, used in pancakes, muffins, or bread, and can also be ground into flour. Steel-cut oats are a chewier and heartier, less processed option.

1 cup water
½ cup rolled or steel cut oats
Pinch of salt
2 T. butter
2 tsp. brown sugar
Dash of cream or milk
½ banana, sliced, or ¼ cup berries (optional)
¼ tsp. ground cinnamon or nutmeg (optional)

Bring water to a boil in a small saucepan. Stir in oats and a pinch of salt. Place a lid on the saucepan, reduce the heat to low, and allow to cook for 7 to 8 minutes. Remove lid and take off heat.

Stir in butter, brown sugar, and dash of cream or milk until combined. Add fruit if desired.

Yield: 1 to 2 servings

How to Cook Outdoors with a Dutch Oven

Many older recipes will take advantage of simmering and Dutch ovens instead of using a regular oven. The pioneers could still prepare many of their favorite dishes using their open campfires, coals, and Dutch ovens, even though they weren't in their regular kitchens with a wood stove and oven. When the power goes out today, there is nothing as lovely as being equipped with skillet or stovetop recipes, and, of course, a wood stove or outdoor burner. This is also true if your oven goes out or is otherwise occupied with another dish.

One of our favorite family activities when we're camping is to have a Saturday night Dutch oven cook-off potluck. So, if you're walking through a campground and see 4 or 5 Dutch ovens lined up, you'll know it's us. We go cooking-show style and judge which dish is the best for the night, which means we get to eat everyone else's food— and when there's a competition involved, everyone brings their best recipes. Score!

When cooking on an open fire, keep a few things in mind. First, you're not actually cooking over the flames. Flames give off very uneven heat. You're actually after the coals.

You may use wood coals, as this would be traditional, but it's easier to use charcoal, especially when you're first learning. Make sure you use charcoal that has not been treated with lighter fluid. Even though your food is enclosed inside the cast iron Dutch oven, you still don't want those fumes if you can help it.

You'll want to get a spider Dutch oven if you plan on doing outdoor cooking. A spider Dutch oven has three legs on it. This helps you to set your pot over the coals and it won't tip as easily. If you happen to have a Dutch oven without the legs, you can still use it outdoors by finding three rocks and creating a tripod for it to sit on.

Make sure you pick a fire pit, gravel, or sandy area where your hot coals won't be a fire hazard and avoid tall dry grass or brush in your area.

When cooking outdoors, you need to plan ahead in order to preheat your oven. It's not like turning on a knob or pushing a button inside the house. You need to light your coals about 15 to 20 minutes before you plan on using them to cook with. You can buy a metal chimney with a handle on it that you pour coals into. Set the filled chimney on top of a paper bag or other tinder material. Light the tinder material from underneath—the fire will burn up into the chimney and ignite the coals.

When the coals begin to turn gray, you're ready to start cooking. Put a small layer of coals down on the ground to heat and cook the bottom of your food. The Dutch oven will sit on top of these. You'll actually put the majority of the coals on top of the oven. A Dutch oven meant for outdoor cooking has a flat top with a lip on the rim to keep the coals from rolling off. Generally, put a third of your coals underneath the oven and two thirds on the lid. You'll want to place the coals around the outer edge of the lid for best heat distribution.

Place your Dutch oven, with the food inside and the lid on, on top of the hot coals. It will take 15 to 20 minutes for the Dutch oven to fully heat. If it's really cold outside or there's a lot of wind, it will take longer and often require more coals. Placing your Dutch oven inside a campfire ring will help block the wind.

To avoid any hot spots over the coals, you'll want to rotate your Dutch oven lid counterclockwise a quarter turn and the Dutch oven pot clockwise a quarter turn every 30 minutes or so. But if you get involved in camping fun and forget to turn the lid and pot, it still turns out fine. There's a lot of forgiveness in this cooking technique!

If you're cooking a dish that requires more than an hour of cooking time, you'll need to start a second batch of coals and add new ones for heat. You'll see the old coals burn down to ash.

Remember, it's easier to add more heat than it is to cool down, especially when we're talking cast iron, which is more efficient at retaining heat than regular metal pots and pans. Start with a smaller amount of coals and add more if necessary to reach the desired temperature.

To determine how many coals you need, the general rule is to take the diameter of your Dutch oven and double it. We never figure it out by math anymore or look up the chart, but you may find this handy until you've gained more experience. I recommend using about 5 more coals than you think you'll need so you have extra you can add, if need be, that are already heated.

Below is a chart to use for the size of Dutch oven and the desired temperature range. These are approximate because cooking outdoors is an adventure, and temperatures fluctuate. If it's cold and windy, you'll need more coals to reach the same temperature. If it's in the middle of August on a scorching afternoon, you'll probably need fewer. Don't worry, there's room for experimentation. If your food isn't cooking fast enough, add more coals. Cooking too fast, pull off some of the coals. You've got this.

Dutch Oven Size	325°	350°	375°	400°	425°	450°
Total number of coals for **8-inch oven**	15	16	17	18	19	20
Coals on top/bottom for **8-inch oven**	10/5	11/5	11/6	12/6	13/6	14/6
Total number of coals for **10-inch oven**	19	21	23	25	27	29
Coals on top/bottom for **10-inch oven**	13/6	14/7	16/7	17/8	18/9	19/10

Total number of coals for **12-inch** oven	23	25	27	29	31	33
Coals on top/bottom for **12-inch** oven	16/7	17/8	18/9	19/10	21/10	22/11
Total number of coals for **14-inch** oven	30	32	34	36	38	40
Coals on top/bottom for **14-inch** oven	20/10	21/11	22/12	24/12	25/13	26/14

The suggested coal amount and ratio above is more along the lines for baking and mimicking your oven at home. For simmering and stewing like a regular stove top, you'll put almost all your coals on the bottom and just a few on the lid. For browning meat (tacos are a favorite outdoor food in the heat of summer with fresh garden veggies) or general frying, put all of your coals on the bottom to concentrate the heat.

Dutch Oven Pizza

Want to bake pizza in a Dutch oven? Of course—especially on those hot summer nights when you don't want to turn on the oven.

Start your coals before you begin assembling your toppings and rolling out your dough so they have time to get hot and sizzling (and your kitchen is staying nice and chill). I recommend using a 10-inch oven if you have it for this at the 425° mark, but the smaller 8-inch or larger 12-inch ovens will work too.

I bake deep-dish pizzas in the house in my 9-inch cast iron skillet and don't use parchment paper, but I recommend lining your Dutch oven with it for cooking pizza outdoors. Parchment makes it easier to pull the pizza up and cut it when done.

Roll out the dough and transfer it to the Dutch oven, pushing it down in the center and letting the dough come up the sides to create a good deep bed for all the fixings. Top with your favorite sauce and toppings. Put on the lid.

Place coals (take into account your outside temperature and weather and adjust accordingly) on the ground or in your designated cooking area. Put your Dutch oven on top of the coals and place the remaining coals on the top of the lid.

Check the pizza after 20 to 25 minutes (remember, it takes about 15 minutes for it to preheat). If the bottom seems too hot (burning crust on the bottom), remove some of the bottom coals. If the cheese isn't beginning to melt, add more coals to the top and continue baking. Check in another 10 minutes or so. When cheese is melted and bubbly, remove the lid and with your pot lifter or a good set of potholders, remove the Dutch oven from the coals. Remember, the entire oven will be hot. Place in a safe area, allow to cool, and enjoy your pizza!

Chapter 3

Culture

June sun bathed the pasture and yard surrounding our homestead. Plants stretched toward the light, leaves unfurling to the warmth and roots burying deep in the rich soil. Insects buzzed about the blossoms.

My gaze fell on the weeds competing with the vegetables. Inside, a load of laundry waited to be hung on the line and another to be folded. Breakfast dishes needed to be washed and supper needed to be prepped. Two blog posts and a magazine article were due.

Meanwhile, a cacophony of squawking and flapping of white feathers reminded me that the meat chickens needed to be fed, watered, and moved to fresh grass before I left for work. I needed to check the pigs' and cattle's water, too, and I couldn't ignore the blocks of weeds and buttercups encroaching on the flower beds. The raspberries would need to be picked this weekend.

Exhaustion rolled over me, like the hot air from the oven on baking day. The urge to lie down in the middle of the patio and sleep almost won. How could I be this tired when I'd just gotten out of bed?

I'm normally energized by the new crops and promise of harvest. But this season the new growth mocked me. Weariness snaked through every fiber of my body, and I forced myself to gather the kids up and drop them off at my mom's before heading off to work. Over my lunch break I sat in my car at the local library, hoping to make a dent in my writing projects during the 30 minutes I had to myself.

A friend pulled up and I rolled down the window. After exchanging greetings she paused and looked at me. "Are you okay? You look really tired."

Tears threatened. That isn't something a woman normally likes to hear, but relief welled up in me. "I *am* tired," I said. "I've been tired for months." My sleep and diet were as they should be, but this tiredness was different. It was an exhaustion without reason. It settled deep in my bones and seemed to mount every day. Growing like the weeds in my garden.

By the grace of God and sheer force of will, I waded through the day. That weekend I got to connect with a dear friend I hadn't seen in more than six months. Upon seeing me, she said. "What happened to your hair?"

I fingered the edges of my hair. It had once been almost waist-length, but now the wispy strands barely brushed the tops of my shoulders. "It's really thin now, isn't it?"

Sometimes God uses other people to help us realize we need to take a new direction. At my friend's urging, I made an appointment to see the doctor. Through lab work, we discovered my thyroid wasn't functioning normally.

I was tired due to the low function of my thyroid and adrenal glands, but there were other factors at play. If you've ever thought, *If one more thing is added to my plate I'll break,* or, *I can't go on like this,* something has to give, my friend.

We need to take a closer look at the culture we're living in. Today's society is very different from the culture of even our mothers' time, let alone our grandparents' and great-grandparents'. With the advent of the Internet and social media, we have more information being thrown at us than ever before—than ever before in the history of mankind. Of course, this has huge benefits (how often have you needed to Google something and found the information in seconds?), but there are other results as well. One of them is the pressure to keep up with everything we see other people doing. The picture-perfect meals, the beautifully designed homes, the carefully put together outfits, the latest achievements of so-and-so. Many times this leaves us feeling like we're not measuring up. We feel like we're lacking.

So what do we do? We put more on our to-do-list and demand more of ourselves, never realizing we're setting ourselves up for failure. Case in point: I have one day off during the work week. On this day, the kids are at school and my husband is at work. This is the day I plan to deep-clean the house, film videos or shoot photos for my website, complete large chunks of writing, and cook a big enough meal that we'll have leftovers for the next night. I bake snacks and fix lunches I wasn't able to do over the weekend, plus—depending on the season—grow, harvest, and preserve our own food.

On one particular day I started out with a long to-do list. It included laundry, cooking supper, baking bread for the week, picking berries and canning a batch of jam (along with having all the dishes and kitchen cleaned afterward), writing an article and editing photos for a recipe tutorial, and cleaning both bathrooms. Did I mention I also have Tuesday night Bible study on this day?

I don't need to tell you I didn't manage all of that. I lamented to my mom that I hadn't accomplished everything I wanted to that day. She asked what items I had on my list I hadn't been able to get to. After reading it off, she said, "No one could get all of that done in a day."

We live in a culture that tells us to hurry up and do more. But that is not what God intended for us. Part of my exhaustion was due to my thyroid issue, yes, but I was expecting more of myself than was humanly possible. I needed to give myself a break.

The more frazzled and exhausted we feel, the less time we have for listening to the still, small voice of the Lord, and the quicker we are to snap at our loved ones. We create a culture of stress and defeat, of impatience and shortness—manifested not only in our minds, but in our attitudes and responses toward those we love. When I'm running around on empty and in a hurry, I'm not usually fond of anything that upsets the already precarious balance I'm foolishly trying to carry.

Culture means *to maintain in conditions suitable for growth*. In order to grow and maintain good health we need adequate sleep, balanced nutrition, interaction with the world around us, and love. But that doesn't account for the health and well-being of our mind and soul. We're often so entrenched in our daily lives, with more on our to-do lists than there are hours in the day, that we're left feeling frazzled and unsettled. We forget to *culture* our mind, attitudes, and soul for growth. We've got to make the decision to cultivate a culture that maintains conditions suitable for growth.

Well, that sounds all fine and dandy, but how does one actually do it?

> Do not conform to the pattern of this world, but be trans-
> formed by the renewing of your mind. Then you will be
> able to test and approve what God's will is—his good,
> pleasing and perfect will (Romans 12:2).

We need to renew our minds from the things that cloud our vision of what is truly important. When we're bogged down with everything we need to get done in a day, we lose the ability to test and approve what God's will is for our life. The world will tell us to do more, to make sure we're measuring up to impossible standards, but God will tell us to rest in Him.

When I was in the midst of my exhaustion and helplessness, I actually wept when I read this verse one morning:

> Come to me, all you who are weary and burdened, and I
> will give you rest. Take my yoke upon you and learn from
> me, for I am gentle and humble in heart, and you will find
> rest for your souls. For my yoke is easy and my burden is
> light (Matthew 11:28-30).

I yearned for rest. Physically and mentally.

Jesus promised it to His children. And He never makes a promise He doesn't keep.

When I wake up now, no matter how I'm feeling, but especially if I'm feeling tired, I offer a simple prayer: "Lord, help me to get done what I need to today and nothing more. Let me seek You first, and give me the wisdom and strength to do what You would have me to do, and to be able to see what that is."

Not only does God answer the prayers of His children, but He grants each of us enough strength to get everything accomplished we need to in a day if we're truly doing His will.

Instead of carrying the heavy banner of *I can't do one more thing*, I can lift up the truth of God's Word. I can do what the Lord has set forth for me today in His strength, and so can you.

But when looking at what we're going to do for the day, we've got to do some pruning. We're getting out those shears and getting this tree into shape. Decide what things truly have to be done for the day and prune off the rest.

I break down my priorities like this:

I know if I don't feed my body nourishing food that I make at home, my health is at risk due to the cellular damage to my esophagus and upper stomach from years of acid reflux. Not only is my health at risk, but so is my budget. There is a definite cost to sacrificing my time to other activities and not planning out my meals and preparing them at home from real food ingredients.

If I don't get our crops planted, harvested, and preserved, my grocery budget goes up. My family and my health need to come before the website, blog, and articles.

Next, I look at the items I need to get done in order to meet my obligations to readers, publishers, and other partners in regard to my writing and podcast. These need to come before any other online work or writing.

While your list might not include the writing and home business aspect, prioritizing things definitely helps me focus on what has to get done, instead of a long list of everything that overwhelms. Take the time to go over everything you're doing in a day and week. Pray over it and then get to work pruning.

* * *

The way people lived before we had supermarkets on every corner and drive-through convenience beckons to me like a lazy river on a hot August day. We make it a goal to practice as many old-fashioned or traditional ways of life as possible on our homestead. One of those traditional practices is making cultured foods.

Cultured foods have been around for thousands of years. It's only in more recent years that modern homes have lost this old-fashioned way of cooking and preparing foods.

What is a cultured food? Cultured foods go through some type of fermentation process, which allows the good and beneficial bacteria to grow and sustain life, while preserving the shelf life of the food and making it healthier for us.

Cultured foods include raw apple cider vinegar, milk and water kefir, yogurt, sour cream, buttermilk, cream cheese, sauerkraut, fermented pickled vegetables, and sourdough. Not all sour cream, buttermilk, and cream cheese still contain the live beneficial bacteria. If you're buying store bought, you'll need to look for live cultures on the labeling, and even then, they can still have additives.

You can't get much more homemade or old-fashioned than cultured foods. You'll even see accounts in the Bible of fermented foods!

Most of us today think of yeast as the dried grains or flakes found in the little packets or jars on store shelves. But yeast in that form is relatively new. Did you know that the shelf-stable yeast purchased in the store was first developed during World War II? How quickly we as a society forsake a time-honored tradition for something fast and easy! It's a shame, because fermented and cultured foods contain good bacteria that our bodies can be lacking. Many of us are lacking a proper balance of gut flora, and the consumption of good lactobacilli can help support intestinal health. Fermented foods also help break down the enzymes in food, making it easier for us to digest and allowing our bodies to absorb more of the nutrients from the food we eat.

Sourdough, often referred to as wild or natural yeast, is one of the oldest forms of baking there is. Many pioneers would take their jar or crock of sourdough with them on the long trek across the prairies or through the mountain passes to go north to Alaska during the gold rush years. In fact, some accounts tell of miners who would sleep with their sourdough to keep it from freezing. While I do love my sourdough, I'm certainly glad I don't have to take it to bed with me.

Sourdough's effectiveness depends on the combination of yeast and lactobacilli. The yeast feeds and creates carbon dioxide and ethanol. The lactobacilli feed on the ethanol, and this creates lactic acid. The bubbles of the carbon dioxide create the pockets in the dough that cause it to rise, while the lactic acid keeps other unwanted organisms at bay and acts as a preservative. Pretty cool, huh?

This is also why when you're using your sourdough to bake products that need to rise, like bread, you need to do it in its active time, after it's recently been fed and is creating lots of bubbles. We'll go into more detail within specific recipes.

Grains and wheat contain phytic acid. It's thought by many that phytic acid prevents us from absorbing phosphorous and also binds to other minerals like calcium, zinc, iron, and magnesium. However, by soaking the flour when you make sourdough, the phytic acid level is lowered, allowing your body to better absorb the needed minerals in the food you're making. When we fast track the production of our food, we miss critical steps that affect our health. Can you tell why I love sourdough?

You'll find many recipes for beginning a sourdough starter, but I didn't want to use any recipes that called for added sugar or store-bought yeast. I was determined to start my sourdough starter the way the pioneers did.

It's amazingly simple to do. All you need is a glass jar, water, and flour. Wild yeast lives in the air around us, and we're simply going to capture it for our sourdough. You can also purchase sourdough starters online. Each area has different yeasts that naturally grow and live there, so you'll see sourdough starters listed by names such as San Francisco or Alaskan Starter. One of the benefits of purchasing a starter is you know you're getting a live culture and you may pick the exact "flavor," so to speak. Either way you decide to go is just fine, but you'll find the instructions below for starting your own sourdough starter from scratch.

You can use any flour of your choice, but I believe you'll have the most luck with a whole wheat flour or rye. I grind my own flour at home and have used organic hard white wheat, hard red wheat, and spelt flour for my starter. If you don't grind your own, I'd recommend a local stone-ground whole wheat flour if possible.

When you first begin your starter, it will require twice-daily feedings for the first few weeks (see optional feeding alternatives if twice a day seems overwhelming). After that it will depend on how much you're using your starter in regard to how often you feed it.

If you find you're not using it often, you can store it in the fridge and feed it once a week.

Sourdough Starter

6 T. flour
¼ cup lukewarm water

I've found a four-cup capacity glass jar works the best for housing my sourdough starter. I prefer to use a Fido jar that has the wire bail and clasp, without the rubber gasket. Because this is a living food, we want it to be able to breathe. You may also use a quart-sized Mason jar (I highly recommend going with the wide mouth on this one) and some cheesecloth or coffee filter, and metal band.

Note: at each feeding you'll be using 6 tablespoons of flour and ¼ cup water.

Day 1

To begin with, place ¼ cup lukewarm water and 6 tablespoons of flour in a clean glass jar. Stir until well combined. Close the lid or the jar *without* the rubber gasket or place a double piece of cheesecloth or coffee filter over the top and secure into place with the metal band.

Place the jar in a warm area where you can keep an eye on it. When first activating your starter, you may find you want to keep it between 68 and 74°. Twelve hours later, check the starter for signs of any bubbles.

Bubbles mean your starter is active, but you'll only see one or two at this point. If you don't see any bubbles, don't panic: just go ahead and add ¼ cup warm water and 6 tablespoons of flour. Stir until combined, scraping the side of the jar. Cover and let rest.

Day 2

Morning: You should see some signs of activity in your starter—either little bubbles on the sides of the jar or on the top of the sourdough starter. Feed the starter. Remember to scrape the sides of the jar to incorporate all the starter when stirring.

12 hours later, feed the starter.

Days 3

Morning: Remove half of the starter from the jar and either put it in your compost pile or in the garbage (it will smell sour and attract fruit flies if you have any, so take care if it's the garbage inside the house). You don't want your starter to outgrow your jar, and it's not strong enough to use yet. Feed the starter.

12 hours later, feed the starter.

Days 4 through 7

Stir and feed your starter morning and evening or every 12 hours.

Continue to feed the starter in this pattern for a week, removing some when there isn't enough room in the jar for the starter to rise after feedings. By the end of the week you should see lots of bubbles and the starter should be rising a few hours after it is fed.

If you don't see any bubbles after three days, you'll need to throw it out and start over.

It's best to store your starter where you'll see it to help you remember to feed it. I leave mine on the kitchen counter next to the sink.

Alternative Feeding Schedule

Think there's no way you can do the twice-daily feeding? Many people have had success with once-daily feedings with a larger quantity of flour and water. If feeding once a day use ½ cup warm water and ¾ cup of flour.

You can try this method, but if you don't see much activity, you may want to switch back to the twice-a-day feeding schedule.

Troubleshooting

- If you see a clear or light brown liquid on top of your starter, pour it off the top and feed your starter. This is called hooch, and it's a sign your starter has run out of food and either needs to be fed more often or a larger amount.

- Your starter isn't rising very much. Try feeding it a little bit more at each feeding and make sure it's in a warm area if your home is cold.

- You forgot to feed your starter and there's a grayish layer of liquid on top. As long as there's not mold growing on it, drain off the liquid and scrape off the top layer of the sourdough starter. Feed it twice a day for a few days, and it should be right as rain.

Let's get ready to put that sourdough to use!

When the starter is a week old, you can begin baking items that don't require doubling as bread does. Pancakes, waffles, and tortillas are three of our favorite sourdough recipes.

The general rule of thumb is that your sourdough starter should be strong enough to bake bread between two and three weeks of life. However, I sometimes find that it takes about two months before my sourdough starter really has full power.

Two of the easiest recipes to start with are sourdough pancakes and waffles. Because I keep my sourdough starter on the thick side, you'll see we don't add any flour to the batter. Just remember to always leave ¼ cup of the sourdough starter in your container so you have enough to build your starter back up with.

Sourdough Pancakes

This recipe was adapted from *Simply Sourdough: The Alaskan Way.*

2 cups sourdough starter

2 T. melted butter, coconut oil, or avocado oil

3 T. yogurt or kefir

3 T. brown sugar

1 egg

1 tsp. baking soda

½ tsp. salt

1 tsp. vanilla

½ tsp. cinnamon or nutmeg

Mix all of the ingredients together.

Heat a cast iron skillet on medium-low heat and pour batter into desired shape and size for pancakes. Makes approximately nine 6-inch pancakes.

Yield: 8 to 10 servings

Sourdough Waffles

I like to make up a big batch of waffles and then freeze some of them for mornings when we're pushed for time. I place waffles on a cookie sheet in a single layer and flash freeze them for an hour. Transfer waffles to a freezer container. When ready to eat, place frozen waffle in a toaster oven to reheat.

2 cups sourdough starter

1 T. melted coconut oil or butter, avocado oil

¼ cup yogurt, applesauce, or cooked pumpkin (this gives it a fun, seasonal variety as well)

3 T. brown sugar

2 eggs
1 tsp. baking soda
½ tsp. salt
1 tsp. vanilla
½ tsp. cinnamon

Mix all of the ingredients together and pour onto a preheated waffle griddle. This is delightful with maple syrup or applesauce. Homemade sweetened whipped cream would also be nice, or maybe pumpkin or apple butter as well.

Yield: 8 to 10 full waffles (with 8 x 9 waffle maker)

Sourdough Tortillas

⅔ cup sourdough starter
2 cups flour (more if needed)
2 heaping tsp. baking powder
½ tsp. sea salt
¼ cup water

Measure out dry ingredients into a mixing bowl. Add the sourdough starter (it does not need to be in an active state) and water. Depending upon the thickness of your sourdough starter (its level of hydration) you may need to add a few more tablespoons of water or flour to get the dough to come together. Don't overmix; stir just until it's combined.

Cover the bowl with a towel and let sit on the counter for 5 to 8 hours. Letting the mixture sit for a longer time allows the sourdough to break down more of the phytic acid in the flour, but it also creates a sourer flavor. My children aren't overly found of the sour part (I happen to love a good sourdough bread), so when I'm making this for the whole family, I generally go with the shorter souring time.

Form into 6 balls of dough. On a lightly floured surface, flatten the dough ball with the palm of your hand. Form into a rustic circle. Fry in hot oil for about 1 minute each side until golden brown. Dry on a plate lined with an absorbent towel.

Yield: 6 8-inch tortillas

Sourdough Pie Crust

> **1¾ cups all-purpose flour or whole wheat pastry (or 2¼ cups spelt flour)**
> **1½ tsp. sugar**
> **1 tsp. salt**
> **¾ cup + 2 T. cold butter**
> **1 cup sourdough starter**

In a large bowl mix together the flour, sugar, and salt. The secret to flaky pie crusts is having the butter melt as it's baking, not when you're handling it. Take the cold butter and cut the stick lengthwise and then into smaller chunks, handling it as little as possible. I've tried grating frozen butter in, but I prefer larger chunks of butter, both in flavor and texture.

Using a pastry cutter or two forks, cut the cold butter into the flour mixture until it resembles little peas.

Add the sourdough starter and stir just until the dough holds together. You may add a teeny bit of cold water if needed (if using whole wheat, you generally need to add more water) but remember, just until it holds together. This will depend on the hydration, or wetness, of your sourdough starter.

Cover the bowl and let the dough rest for 5 to 7 hours. An hour before using, chill in the fridge for at least an hour.

Divide dough into half. If only using one crust, wrap the other half tightly in plastic wrap and freeze until ready to use.

To use, lightly flour your work surface and rolling pin. Roll to ¼-inch thick and place in pie plate. Crimp edges and use in your favorite quiche or pie recipes.

Yield: 2 single-crust pie shells

Baking Bread and Rolls with Sourdough

A few things you need to know when baking bread with sourdough as your main leavening agent: Store-bought yeast works very fast—one of the reasons that specific strain of yeast was chosen. But the natural yeast in the sourdough has different strains and takes longer to rise. Plan for at least 4 to 8 hours of rise time on your sourdough products.

One of the benefits of this longer rise time is that the additional flour you add to the dough ingredients with the starter will have time for the bacteria to begin to break down the phytic acid and aid in digestion. Most traditional food experts recommend 7 to 12 hours for the phytic acid to be broken down, or longer. However, if you or your family are not particularly fond of a really tangy (nice way of saying "sour") flavor, you'll want to use the shorter rise and souring time.

With the sourdough, or natural, yeast, you can either do a single rise or a double rise. I've found the single rise works best when your starter is younger and not as strong and you don't want the stronger taste. It generally takes about 4 to 6 hours, so you don't have the full souring time and therefore not as much of the phytic acid is broken down.

The double rise is like working with store-bought yeast in that you will punch it down, form your rolls or bread, and allow the dough to double in size again, except your time between rises is much longer, about 4 to 6 hours for each rise, and the result will have a stronger sour taste. Either option is fine. I usually go with the single rise as I get a higher rise and my kids don't like the stronger flavor of a double rise. Personally, I love a good tang on the bread, but the goal is for my entire family to eat and enjoy it.

Remember, your sourdough starter will need to be at least several weeks old before you rely solely on it as the leavening agent in your bread. Your starter will also need to be in its active state. Sourdough starter is in its active state a few hours after feeding when there are bubbles and it's beginning to rise or double in size. The starter should be almost doubling in size about four hours after feeding. You can mark the level on the outside of your jar, feed it, and then see how much it rises above it. This will let you know how strong and active it is and approximately how much time passed from feeding until it became active.

Care of Your Sourdough Starter

Once your new sourdough starter is established, there are two methods to keeping it alive. One is to leave it out on your counter, feeding it twice a day in the same routine you used when creating it. This is great if you're using it almost daily or at least every two days. If you find yourself only using it once a week or wanting to take a break from it for vacation or other reasons (ain't no shame in that), then you'll want to use method two.

The second method is to feed the starter and then immediately after feeding put it in the fridge. The cold greatly slows down the activity of the bacteria and allows you to leave it in the fridge for at least a week before feeding it again. I confess, sometimes I've forgotten mine in the way back corner of the fridge for almost a month between feedings.

If you forget for a long period of time, you will find a very dark, almost black layer of liquid on the top. Drain it off, scrape off the top layer of your sourdough, and feed it. Leave it out on the counter for a few days and feed it every 12 hours. Sourdough is amazingly adaptive.

I usually bounce between both methods, depending upon the season I'm in. The summer months are filled with canning, gardening, and harvesting, so I don't bake nearly as much. This is when I use the refrigeration method primarily. Come fall I'll leave it out for a few weeks during baking sprees and then put it back in hibernation for a bit. Choose whatever works best for you at the time.

When using the refrigerator method, bring your sourdough starter out of the cold two to three days before you want to bake bread and feed your starter every 12 hours. On the day of baking, feed the starter, and when you see it begin to rise (usually 2 to 3 hours after feeding) begin making your recipe.

For many people, the goal of having a sourdough starter is to not rely on store-bought yeast and for the health benefits. However, I've come to learn that my desire for my family to be healthier and more self-sufficient (and cutting out an ingredient is saving money) doesn't do any of us any good if they don't like the food and don't want to eat it.

If you're just switching from regular store-bought bread, I suggest starting with the following bread recipe first. Our goal is for you to have success right off the bat, with both the bread and your family's taste buds, so you'll be more likely to keep with it.

This recipe uses some store-bought yeast with the sourdough starter, which means you can technically try this one out even if your starter isn't quite mature enough yet to work fully on its own. Best part, it's so delicious they'll think they're still eating regular old white bread, but you and I will keep the secret—it's actually sourdough.

I first got this recipe from a dear gentleman. His sourdough starter had died, and he heard I had an active one. I shared a cup of my starter with him and he brought me a loaf of this bread. My family may have almost swooned when they ate it.

Of course, I asked for his recipe and he shared it with me. It was a copy of the Sourdough White Bread recipe from Patrick McManus's *Whatchagot Stew: A Memoir of an Idaho Childhood with Recipes and Commentaries,* but he'd altered the recipe to the loaf he'd given me. Is it just me, or does anyone else love seeing handwritten notes on a recipe?

I altered it slightly from the original recipe he'd given me (making this recipe twice altered and once removed) as it called for powdered milk and I generally don't have that on hand. This is the beauty of recipes—we get to tweak them to make them our own. I've also included notes on how to check if the dough is ready and forming loaves if you're newer to bread making or need a brushup.

Sourdough White Bread

3 tsp. sugar
2 ¼ tsp. active dry yeast
1⅔ cups warm water
⅓ cup milk
1 tsp. salt
2 T. melted butter
2 cups sourdough starter
6 cups all-purpose flour

In a large mixing bowl combine sugar, yeast and warm water (not hot as that will kill the yeast, but lukewarm); stir and let sit for about 5 minutes until it turns foamy. Add milk, salt, melted butter, sourdough starter, and 2 cups of the flour. If you have a mixer, mix dough and continue adding ½ cup flour at a time until it's kneadable. Knead for 8 minutes.

If you're doing this by hand the old-fashioned way, continue stirring and adding in the flour until it's smooth enough to handle. Turn out onto a floured surface and knead by hand until dough is smooth, about 8 to 10 minutes.

Place dough in a greased bowl, cover with a towel, and place in a warm area. Allow dough to double in size, about an hour or so usually.

Punch dough down.

Take out two standard-sized bread pans and either grease them well (we seem to be a society that is afraid of fat—but don't skimp on the greasing or your loaf will stick to the pan) or line them with parchment paper. I reuse the same piece of parchment paper multiple times with bread.

Lightly flour hands and counter. Divide dough in two and pat one piece into a rectangle on the counter—measure the narrow end of your rectangle to the long side of your loaf pan (this will ensure it fits perfectly into your loaf pan). Roll it up from the narrow end, take the two ends of the roll, lightly tuck them up under the roll, and place the loaf in the bread pan. Repeat with the other dough ball.

Cover with a towel and allow to double in size. This usually takes anywhere from an hour to an hour and a half.

Preheat oven to 400°. Bake loaves 25 to 30 minutes. You can test if a loaf is done by thumping the top of the bread—it should have a hollow sound when finished.

Remove loaves from oven and immediately slather the top with some butter. Don't be afraid of too much butter—there is no such thing. Allow to cool for about 15 minutes in the pan, then remove to a cooling rack. Wait at least another 15 minutes before slicing.

Sourdough Sandwich Bread

This is a true sourdough bread recipe, meaning there is no store-bought yeast and it takes close to eight hours of rising time for the natural yeast to do its work. I adapted my regular whole wheat honey buttermilk sandwich loaf to this one. We don't need the buttermilk in this recipe, however, because the sourdough itself will act as our acidic ingredient.

Remember, working with sourdough is an art form, and you'll get it down. Depending upon the hydration level of your sourdough and the warmth of your room, you may need to adjust both the amount of liquid and the time frame.

When doing a risen bread product like rolls and bread, you'll want your sourdough to be in its active state. Feed it morning and night a few days before using. Feed it a few hours before making the dough.

If you're using all-purpose flour you may need to increase the measurement to 7 cups, but start with 6. This recipe makes two standard loaves.

> **2 cups sourdough starter**
> **1½ cups water**
> **¼ cup honey**

1 T. sea salt

1 egg

6 T. melted butter

5 to 6 cups spelt (spelt requires more flour than
regular wheat) or whole wheat flour

In a large mixing bowl or your stand mixer bowl, stir together everything but the flour. If grinding your own flour at home, you'll get a lighter bread if you sift it, so sift your flour. Mix in 1 cup flour at a time on low speed, or stir by hand.

When all the flour is added, knead with attachment or by hand for 5 minutes. The trick to keeping whole wheat bread soft is to not add too much flour. The dough should be sticky and climb up the dough hook.

If using fresh-ground flour, let the dough sit for 10 minutes to continue soaking up the moisture. Knead for 4 more minutes, adding slightly more flour if needed in order to handle the dough.

Cover with a towel and let dough rise in a warm spot (the oven with the light on works great) for three to four hours.

Lightly oil the counter and grease your loaf pans. Divide dough in half and roll out one dough ball into a rectangle. Form into a loaf and place inside prepared bread pans, repeat with the other half of the dough. Allow to rise until doubled, which can take anywhere from 3 to 5 hours. To encourage a last bit of burst in height, preheat the oven to 400° with the bread in the oven. This extra heat will make it shoot upward.

Bake for 10 minutes then turn the oven down to 375° for another 10 to 15 minutes. Take the bread out of the oven and remove the loaves from the bread pans to a wire rack. Slather with butter and let cool.

Alternative rise: If you'd rather not have the longer rising time but still want to use all traditional sourdough, form the loaves from the get go and let them rise until doubled in the bread pans and then bake. This works well for a shorter rise time and if your sourdough starter isn't very strong yet.

Fermented Foods

One of the earliest forms of food preservation and preparation known to man is fermentation. Before the advent of refrigeration, freezing, and even canning, fermentation was a way to keep perishable foods longer and to add flavor. However, there are even more benefits to fermented and cultured foods than that.

All my fellow Laura Ingalls Wilder fans will remember the talk of barrels or crocks of pickles. Some of you may even remember your grandparents or great-grandparents having crocks, or large Mason jars, full of saltwater brine pickles, where just the vegetable, salt, and water were used to make a pickle. You're about to learn how to make them yourself, and as much as I love my home-canned pickles, there's a beauty to the fermented ones you'll want to try.

One of the great things about saltwater-brined (fermented) pickles is you can make as little or as much as you'd like at a time. Truth be told, you could do that with canned pickles, but I'm not about to go through all that work and heating up my water bath canner for one jar of pickles. When I have a small harvest of produce, I will ferment it.

If you're new to fermented pickles, don't expect them to taste exactly like a vinegar pickle. They're similar but have their own unique flavor. The best part about them is that they're teeming with beneficial microcultures and bacteria that help to limit pathogenic bacteria in our immune system. The enzymes in fermented food actually help predigest the food so that our bodies are better able to absorb the vitamins and minerals.

- -

Fermented Pickles

You'll need the following supplies to get started:

Glass Jar or Fermenting Crock: I personally prefer to use a Mason jar for all of my fermenting except for sauerkraut. Wide mouth is best so you can fit the fermenting weight inside with ease.

Water: I use our well water, which is considered hard. Though hard water isn't desired by most experts, I haven't had any issues. Filtered or distilled water is recommended, but tap water will work if you have a filter.

Salt: Unrefined sea salt with no additives is recommended. Though canning salt doesn't have additives in it, it doesn't have all of the minerals that unrefined sea salt does. We want to give our microcultures as much food as possible. Gray, red, and pink sea salts are fine—just make sure you read the ingredients label for any additives, and stay away from those.

Weight: You'll need some type of weight to keep the pickles beneath the brine level. You can purchase fermenting weights or use any clean weight that will fit inside the jar. I've used old baby food jars filled with a bit of the pickling liquid to act as a weight.

Optional but highly recommended:

I know our ancestors didn't have these, but since this is a modern guide to old-fashioned living, I highly recommend getting an airlock system for fermenting. My first summer of fermenting I didn't have an airlock system. I ended up losing gallons of pickles due to an overgrowth of mold. Please, let me save you the headache.

Airlock systems are fairly inexpensive and you'll use them over and over again. They allow the gasses from the fermentation to escape without allowing oxygen and yeast in, which result in an overload of bad microorganisms to the good and a mold overgrowth. I have both a Perfect Pickler® System and Zatoba-Kraut Kaps®.

Sauerkraut is one fermented vegetable I didn't need to use an airlock system on in order to have success.

To make the brine, pour 2 tablespoons of salt into 4 cups (1 quart) of barely warm water. Stir until salt is completely dissolved.

Take fresh, rinsed, and clean vegetables and pack them into your clean container to a 2-inch headspace (the space between the top of the vegetables and the very top of the jar).

Pour the brine over the vegetables to a 1-inch headspace. You want to make sure the vegetables are completely submerged as any pieces exposed above the brine will mold. Add your weight of choice to the jar to help keep all your veggies beneath the surface. As they ferment they tend to rise.

Place your lid on. If you're using an airlock system, follow the instructions that come with it; if not, use a regular canning lid and band. Just know as the gasses build up, you'll need to "burp" (quickly unscrew the band to release the gasses) every day or so. The disadvantage to this is, no matter how superfast we are, some oxygen will get in, but many people have success with this method.

Put your jar in a warm location but not in direct sunlight. Ideally, 70 ° is best, but down to 65° will do. The colder temperature may require a few extra days of fermentation. However, you don't want the temperature to go above 74°, as warmer temps cause yeast and bad bacteria to take over.

After a day or so, you'll notice the brine will turn cloudy and little bubbles will begin to form. Congratulations, you have fermentation! It's really cool to watch. Allow the vegetables to ferment for 4 days.

After 4 days, go ahead and do a taste test. If they're tangy enough for you, then put a regular metal canning lid and band on and move them to the fridge for long-term storage. If they're not quite there flavor-wise, allow them to continue fermenting up to 10 days—basically, until they taste strong enough to you.

Occasionally, a film will start to form over the top of the brine. Take a spoon and skim off the film. If it's at the end of the ferment, go ahead and put them in the fridge. If they need to continue fermenting, replace the lid and keep fermenting. Most times the film doesn't grow back.

Sometimes a piece of vegetable will rise to the surface, despite the weight. If it's exposed above the brine level, it will begin to discolor and if not removed, it will mold. Remove any pieces that become exposed and reposition your weight.

Once you move the jars to the fridge, fermentation will continue, but the cold slows it down a ton. Fermented vegetables will keep in the fridge for months. They're not considered shelf stable, so don't keep them on the pantry shelf like you would canned pickles. *They must be stored in the fridge.*

I generally let most of my vegetables ferment 7 days for that magic flavor place, but this will depend upon your palate and the warmth of your room.

I prefer most of my pickles to be garlic and dill flavor, especially green beans, green tomatoes, and cucumbers. I add 2 to 3 peeled and smashed cloves of garlic to each quart sized jar (increase ratio according to container size), and 2 heads fresh dill or a tablespoon dried dill, plus your favorite spices. I like a teaspoon of mustard seed, too. Adjust the dill to your taste preferences.

If you're making dilly beans, it's recommended by the Perfect Pickler®, Inc that you blanch them in boiling water for 2 minutes, let cool, and then proceed as normal.

When making fermented cucumber pickles, many people like to add a couple of grape leaves to the jar as it's thought the tannins in the leaf will help create a crisper pickle. Feel free to add your favorite spices like mustard seeds and whole black peppercorns for flavor.

It's also recommended that you always snip off the blossom end of your cucumbers to remove an enzyme that creates mushy pickles. I usually remove both ends to help get the brine down in the cucumber (and in case you're not sure which end was the blossom end if you didn't pick them yourself). Make sure you're choosing fresh pickling cucumbers. Waxy cucumbers or English cucumbers don't make good pickles.

When fermenting bright green vegetables like green beans, cucumbers, and green tomatoes, you'll notice the color change to a duller green as the fermentation takes place. This is normal and just shows the enzymes are doing their work.

Sauerkraut

1 head green or purple cabbage
1 T. sea salt

Sauerkraut can be made with either purple or green cabbage. A fresh head of cabbage is best, because you need the moisture content in the leaves to create your brine.

Using an old earthenware crock works great for sauerkraut, but you can also use a wide mouth Mason jar or even a large glass bowl.

Remove the outer leaves and core of cabbage. Chop or shred into the desired size pieces for your sauerkraut. A food processor can make quick work of the cabbage if you're going for shredded.

Many folks will pound their cabbage to release the juices, but my friend Wardeh Harmon (author of *The Complete Idiot's Guide to Fermenting Foods* and founder of TraditionalCookingSchool.com) shares this method for a no-pound sauerkraut and is what we've always used for ours.

Place the cabbage in a large bowl and sprinkle with 1 tablespoon unrefined sea salt. Let sit for about 30 minutes and then give it a good stir. You'll begin to see juices form, but you need enough liquid to cover the cabbage when it's put in a jar, so stir it up and let it sit for another 30 to 40 minutes. If you have any live cultured sauerkraut already in the fridge, you can use a cup of the brine to help inoculate the new batch.

Instructions for Mason Jar:

Take a clean wide-mouth Mason jar and pack the cabbage tightly into it. Keep pushing down on the cabbage so that the juice rises to cover the surface. If you're not using an airlock system but just a regular canning lid, make sure you burp the jar (untighten the band) to release the gases every so often. You'll see the metal lid start to bulge or become firm if they're starting to build up and know it's time to burp the baby...err, jar. Place the weight inside to keep the cabbage beneath the brine.

Fermenting Crock or Large Bowl Instructions:

You will need a weight to keep the juices above the surface of the cabbage. Use a plate that covers the entire surface area of the crock or bowl. Fill a small Mason jar with water and place it on the plate to act as a weight. Make sure you can see the liquid above the cabbage.

Allow the sauerkraut to ferment for one to two weeks. We've found one week doesn't have that tangy flavor for us, so two weeks is about the sweet spot. Many people believe sauerkraut should ferment for a full four weeks for the maximum amount of good bacteria. This is up to you, but regardless, after it's reached the desired flavor, you must transfer it to the fridge.

If a film develops, you can skim that off. But if you see white or pink mold, you'll need to discard the sauerkraut and start over.

Yield: approximately 4 cups

Yogurt

Most of us are familiar with having yogurt in our home, but many store-bought yogurts aren't very healthy with all of the additives they contain. It's much cheaper and healthier to make homemade yogurt. Do not use ultra-pasteurized milk if you're able, and preferably non-homogenized as well, though if you can't find sources for these, regular milk will work.

4 to 6 cups milk
¼ cup yogurt (with live cultures) or yogurt starter

Pour 4 to 6 cups of milk into a saucepan. On medium-low heat, bring the milk to 160° to 175°. Allowing the milk to heat at 175° for 15 minutes will result in a thicker yogurt. When you heat the milk, a layer of scalded milk will form on top. Skim this off with a spoon.

Allow milk to cool to 110° and pour into a clean Mason jar. Add starter and mix in thoroughly. If you add the culture before the milk is cooled, you'll kill it. If you add the culture into cold milk, you'll also kill it. It just likes to be warm—not hot, not cold. Anyone else thinking of Goldilocks right now?

Put a lid on the jar. I use plastic lids for Mason jars or save ones from peanut butter jars. (I have used a regular canning lid and band, but I prefer to save those for my actual canning.) I tend to use my Mason jars for everything from leftovers to cups on the go, so the plastic lids are great, as keeping track of bands drives me crazy.

Keep yogurt between 100° and 110° for 4 to 6 hours. There are a few ways to keep your yogurt warm. You can purchase a yogurt maker, but I prefer the more frugal route when possible. I've filled my slow cooker with three inches of water and turned it on the "keep warm" setting with the lid off. This setting keeps the water at 110°. Another option is to wrap your jars in a thick bath towel and put them in the oven. The oven works as a natural incubator. Just don't forget your yogurt is in the oven and turn it on! Other people will use a small ice chest, put extra jars of hot water in it, and use it to keep the yogurt warm. All these options work well.

After five hours check to see if yogurt is thick. I let my yogurt ferment for close to a full 24 hours to remove more of the milk sugars. Just remember, the longer it ferments, the tangier it gets. Once it's reached the desired thickness, store the yogurt in the fridge for up to one week—if you don't gobble it up within a day or two.

If your yogurt separates too much, with a lot of whey (watery liquid) on top, then your yogurt was a little too hot while fermenting. Try keeping it slightly cooler. You can either stir the whey back into the yogurt or drain it to use as liquid in cooking or fermenting.

You can use the plain yogurt in place of sour cream and mayonnaise in many cooking and baking recipes. Make sure to save ¼ cup of your fresh yogurt as starter for your next batch. I freeze my starter so I don't have to remember to save it later and so that the starter is at its strongest point, which is right after it's been fed.

If you and your family are used to store-bought yogurt, you will probably need to add some type of sweetener if eating plain.

Sweetener options:
- Drizzle in some raw honey (not for children under a year)
- Maple syrup
- Jam or jelly for a fruity, sweet option
- Stevia extract (I use the liquid version, and it mixes in great)

Master Smoothie Recipe

½ cup yogurt
½ cup water or milk of choice
½ cup frozen or fresh berries or a whole, small peach
or banana
Sweetener of choice to taste (I use 6 drops of liquid
Stevia)
¼ tsp. cinnamon (optional, depending upon fruit)
4 ice cubes

Optional add-ins
- 1 scoop of protein powder of your choice
- ½ scoop of gelatin (I only use organic or grass-fed brands for this)
- 1 T. cooked pumpkin with a dash of nutmeg
- ¼ to ½ cup frozen greens or spinach
- 1 T. almond or peanut butter
- 1 T. cocoa powder
- 1 T. ground flax seed
- 1 T. chia seeds

Place all ingredients in a high-powered blender and blend until smooth and frothy. Pour into a Mason jar and bottoms up!

Yield: approximately 1½ cups

Oatmeal Yogurt Bowl

½ cup water
¼ cup oatmeal (not instant)

½ teaspoon vanilla extract
Pat of butter
¼ cup yogurt
Dash of salt
¼ cup fresh or frozen fruit
Sweetener of choice
Healthy sprinkle of cinnamon
1 T. finely chopped nuts (optional)

For a single serving, bring ½ cup water to a boil in a small saucepan. Stir in oatmeal, reduce heat to low, and cover. Cook for 7 minutes. Remove from heat and stir in vanilla and butter. Then add yogurt, salt, fruit, sweetener of choice, cinnamon, and nuts.

Granola

There's little that goes better with yogurt than granola—it's the creaminess of the yogurt against the crunch of the granola. Granola is extremely easy to make at home.

3 cups oatmeal (not instant)
1 cup chopped nuts (pecans are my favorite)
½ cup honey or maple syrup
2 T. brown sugar (if you're avoiding refined sugar, omit)
¼ cup melted coconut oil or avocado oil
½ tsp. sea salt
1 tsp. vanilla extract
½ tsp. ground cinnamon (optional)
2 cups any combination of the following:
    sunflower seeds
    shredded coconut
    dried fruit of choice

> **extra chopped or ground nuts of choice**
> **mini chocolate chips or chunks (add in after**
> **granola is cooked and cooled, not before)**

Preheat oven to 275°. Mix all of the ingredients together, *except* dried fruit or chocolate, in a large bowl. Pour into a large, rimmed baking sheet.

Bake for 45 to 55 minutes until golden brown and toasted. Stir the granola every 15 to 20 minutes to prevent burning. Take out of the oven, and if you're adding dried fruit, go ahead and mix it all in together.

Allow to cool completely before adding chocolate and storing in an airtight container, if you don't eat it all at once. You can eat it as cereal, mix it in with yogurt, or snitch a few handfuls all by itself.

Yield: 5 to 6 cups (depending on how many add-ins you used)

Buttermilk

Buttermilk is held in high regard by bakers because of the wonderful flaky effect it has on baked goods. The reason for this is the acid, which creates pockets in the dough as it's baking, creating a light, flakier texture.

Buttermilk is the easiest cultured food to make. And it's a lot cheaper to make at home than to buy. One of the great things about cultured buttermilk is you can, of course, use it in your baked goods, though when it's cooked, you're losing the probiotic benefit due to the heat. But it will still treat your baked goods well.

Seriously, if you can pour cold milk in a jar and stir in a ¼ cup of starter, you're good to go. No heating anything up or fishing out any cultures. You can also use cultured buttermilk to just drink straight up (my father's preferred method), in a smoothie, or in homemade ranch dressing (my favorite).

You may use any milk you desire. My grandmother had raw milk, and that's preferred by some, but cost and ease of purchasing raw milk (it's illegal in some states) may not make this an option. I prefer organic nonhomogonized milk, but have had success with regular milk as well. Totally up to you, my friend.

1 quart milk

¼ cup live cultured buttermilk (you can also purchase starter cultures online)

Pour the cold milk into a clean quart-sized Mason jar. Stir in the starter culture or ¼ cup live cultured buttermilk. Cover with cheese-cloth or a coffee filter and secure with a rubber band—or use my go to, a canning metal band. Place in a warm area—around 70° is preferred. Allow to culture for 12 to 18 hours. The colder the room, the longer it will take the culture to set. Check it at 12 hours and see if it's firm. It will look set like yogurt.

Then place in the fridge for 6 to 8 hours to finish up before using. If you want it to be thinner, like milk, stir it briskly. The wonderful thing about cultured milk products is they keep longer. Your buttermilk will be good for 2 to 3 weeks in the fridge. But remember to always reserve ¼ cup for your next batch.

Now be prepared to make the best buttermilk recipes ever. Seriously, if you've used the substitute of lemon or vinegar in milk for buttermilk recipes, ain't nothing compared to the real thing.

Let's get to putting that buttermilk to use, shall we?

Overnight Buttermilk Pancakes

2 cups flour
2 cups buttermilk
4 T. melted butter
½ tsp. sea salt
3 T. brown sugar

1 egg
1 tsp. baking soda
1 tsp. vanilla

The night before, combine the flour and buttermilk, cover the bowl with a towel, and let sit on the counter overnight or 8 to 12 hours. In the morning, stir in butter, salt, sugar, egg, baking soda, and vanilla to the flour and buttermilk. Add a wee bit more buttermilk if batter is too thick.

Heat a griddle or cast iron skillet over medium heat with a teaspoon of butter. When butter is melted and skillet is hot, pour out pancakes to desired size. The batter is a little bit thick, but they make amazingly light and fluffy pancakes.

You can make these straight up in the morning if you want to, without doing the soak. But the overnight soak helps aid digestion.

Yield: 8 servings

Oatmeal Pancakes

Speaking of pancakes and oatmeal, these are one of my absolute favorite pancakes of all time. I've even been known to snitch one off the plate and eat it plain because I simply can't wait to put the toppings on before getting a bite. They're so good they don't need syrup.

This recipe comes from my mother. With the addition of oatmeal, these are higher in both fiber and protein, making them a healthier choice than just a regular pancake recipe.

The recipe below also has a soaked variation. Soaked recipes go back to traditional cooking of sourdough and cultured food—the days before refrigeration. People made buttermilk, yogurt, and kefir because it kept their milk products longer. There are also some health benefits to soaked foods. It's thought that a soaked flour or grain recipe helps break down the phytic acid in the flour and oats, making it easier for us to digest.

For a soaked option, take a cup of yogurt (this replaces one of the cups of milk in the recipe) and mix with 1 cup of milk, 1½ cups oats, and ¾ cup flour in a bowl the night before. Cover with a towel and let sit overnight. In the morning, prepare as normal. You can also use two cups of real cultured buttermilk or dairy kefir.

2 cups milk

1½ cups old-fashioned oats

2 eggs

½ cup melted butter, coconut oil, or avocado oil

¾ cup flour

1 T. brown sugar or omit for sugar free (stevia works well in this)

2½ tsp. baking powder

1 tsp. sea salt

½ tsp. cinnamon

1 tsp. vanilla

Pour milk over oats and let sit 2 minutes. Meanwhile, beat eggs and other liquid ingredients together. Add the rest of the dry ingredients and liquids to the milk and oats. Fry in hot oil, about 2 minutes on each side or until golden brown. Top with warm applesauce, buttermilk syrup (page 28), or jam or jelly of choice.

Yield: 8 to 10 servings

Milk Kefir

If you've never heard of kefir before, don't worry, I had never heard of it either as a child or young adult. Most sources show kefir originated in the North Caucasus Mountains. Kefir look like small grains (but they don't actually contain any grain or gluten) that consist of colonies of good yeast and bacteria, aka probiotics. Kefir grains actually have a much higher amount and more diverse types of the good bacteria and yeast than yogurt—like up to 5 times more.

I'm here to let you in on a little secret, kefir is actually easier to make than yogurt, though it is a daily thing.

If you can get grains from a friend or someone local, that will be your best bet, as you can skip the rehydrating step, and if it's a friend, you generally won't have to buy it. Otherwise I've ordered mine from Cultures for Health online. If you order your grains online they'll come to you dehydrated, which will involve you slowly waking them up over a week until they reach full strength, hence the local recommendation if possible.

Don't worry—if you go the online route they'll come with detailed instructions on how to rehydrate them. That's how I started mine. Once you have plumped and hydrated kefir grains, you're ready to go.

Up to 4 cups of cold milk
1 to 2 tsp. kefir grains

Pour milk into a clean glass jar. Add in the kefir grains and stir with a wooden or plastic spoon. Note: it's recommended to not use aluminum utensils with your kefir.

Cover the jar with cheesecloth or a coffee filter (I think you have the drill down by now) and secure. Set the jar in a warm area, but not in direct sunlight, and allow to culture for 24 hours. You'll notice the milk thickening up.

When my grains were in their infancy, it took them almost 2 weeks before they thickened up the milk in 24 hours, so don't be discouraged if they're a little slow to come to maturity. Just keep changing the milk and give them a little extra time.

If after 24 hours the milk isn't thickening up, let it go another 4 to 8 hours, especially if your kitchen is on the cooler side.

Strain the kefir grains out (pictured above) and start a new batch with fresh milk in a clean jar. Store your freshly made kefir in the fridge or enjoy immediately. You can purchase a small strainer (plastic is advised) or use cheesecloth. If your kefir is thick, it can take a while to strain through. I've found it faster and easier to wash my hands and just fish the grains out with my fingers. Some will be on the bottom while a few are on top, at least with my grains.

The grains do need fresh milk after every fermentation, usually every 24 hours, but if you're going on vacation or need a break, you can feed them fresh milk and put them in the fridge for a week or two. It is hard on them if you do this too frequently, but every now and then should be fine.

Many folks use kefir just like yogurt in smoothies, eating, cooking, and baking. I like to take mine and add ¼ cup fruit or berries to 1 cup of kefir, whirl it in the blender, and let it sit for a few hours before drinking. The fruit sweetens it up a little bit and makes a healthy snack. The extra fermentation makes it slightly effervescent. And come summertime you can use it to make berry kefir popsicles. Yum.

Great Depression-Era Tip

Back in my grandmother's day when they milked the cow every morning, they had gallons of fresh, raw milk. They lived far off the road, down a dirt lane and over a creek. No electricity, which meant no refrigerator, and no indoor bathroom, but a good milk cow. (The outhouse is still standing.)

One of the benefits of culturing your food is it naturally preserves it. During the Great Depression, food wasn't allowed to go to waste. Culturing the cream and milk allowed folks who couldn't afford electricity to keep their dairy products longer. The culturing provides the same benefit for us today. A quart of yogurt or dairy kefir will keep much longer in the fridge than a quart of plain milk.

Sour Cream

We know cultured foods are better for us, and they've proven to be less expensive for me to make at home. Did you know making homemade cultured sour cream is just as easy as making yogurt? Sour cream is thicker because we're using cream, and there's a higher fat content.

You can purchase a sour cream culture starter, but I simply use my yogurt in cream to make sour cream. A dollop on baked potatoes, chili, homemade nachos, scrambled eggs, you name it, and now it contains the goodness of live cultures.

Without a refrigerator, cream and butter would naturally culture. If you have raw cream/milk (which is what my grandparents had back in the day) the making of sour cream is incredibly easy. Note: Option

1 method will only work with raw cream/milk. If the milk has been heated or pasteurized, *you cannot use this method.*

Option 1: Raw Cream

Separate your raw cream from the milk. The cream rises to the top, and is thick and a slightly different color. Spoon it off into a clean Mason jar. Place a layer of cheesecloth or a coffee filter over the top and secure it with a rubber band or canning ring. Let it sit for 24 to 48 hours in a warm area. The warmer your house (think summer months or near a heat source) the faster it will culture.

Option 2: Pasteurized Cream

To make sour cream with store-bought pasteurized cream (I prefer to not use Ultra High Temperature (UHT) treated milk or cream), you'll need cream and some type of starter culture. The good news is you can use either milk kefir or yogurt as your starter.

The reason we heat the milk when making yogurt, sour cream, and cheese is the heat denatures the whey protein, creating a thicker, smoother, and creamier product.

Heat the cream to 180° and then let it cool to about 80° (basically room temperature). Pour the cooled cream into a glass Mason jar and add in 1 tablespoon live culture, either yogurt or milk kefir, to 1 cup cream. Stir and cover with cheesecloth or a coffee filter, secure with a rubber band or metal screw-down band.

Let sit at room temperature for 12 to 24 hours, until you see it's thickened up and set. The longer it cultures, the thicker it will become. Due to using grass-fed cream with all the lovely yellow color, my sour cream isn't white, but a gorgeous buttery color.

Store in the fridge and enjoy your probiotic-rich sour cream! Just remember to save 1 or 2 tablespoons to use in the next batch, or you can keep using your kefir or yogurt.

Homemade Mayonnaise

If you enjoyed the sour cream, wait until you try this mayonnaise! While it's not a cultured recipe, this is a staple in our fridge. And by staple, I mean we're not allowed to run out. My husband eats it on everything. A dollop on top of chili is just the thing, and instead of bread and butter, my husband loves bread and mayonnaise. Let me tell you, don't mess with a man and his mayo.

This was one of the last holdouts of store-bought products, mainly because my husband insisted on a certain brand name and nothing else. I admire his loyalty, but when going over the ingredients list and cost, I was determined to come up with a homemade version. The main ingredient in store bought mayonnaise is soy oil. I have issues with this for a couple of reasons. First, soy is a major genetically modified crop, and the oil is usually hydrogenated. Second, soy contains phytoestrogens and endocrine-disrupting compounds.[1] It tends to be in tons of commercially processed foods, so I try to limit our consumption of it whenever I can.

This version contains only recognizable ingredients, and you can whip up a jar of homemade mayonnaise in less than three minutes. No more running to the store.

1 egg
2 T. vinegar (I use raw apple cider)
1 tsp. lemon juice
¼ tsp. sea salt
Pinch of sugar (optional)
1 cup oil (organic avocado oil is my preferences)

Place 1 egg in the bottom of a pint-sized Mason jar. In a separate bowl, mix together the vinegar, lemon juice, and salt. Add 1 tablespoon of this mixture to the egg.

Place an immersion blender into the bottom of the jar and blend on high for 12 to 15 seconds, until the egg is nice and foamy.

Keeping the blender going, slowly pour in 1 cup of oil. When all the oil is added, pour in the rest of the vinegar mixture.

Keep blending, and within seconds you'll see the oil and egg start to emulsify, turning a thick, creamy white. Continue lifting the immersion blender until all the mayonnaise is emulsified. This really doesn't take very long—barely a minute.

Store the mayonnaise in the fridge.

This has the perfect tang to it. I've tried using olive oil, but found it had too strong of a flavor for our liking.

I know many people are shocked to see a raw egg in mayonnaise, but the addition of the vinegar and lemon juice add acid to help kill bacteria. We use a fresh egg from our chickens, so I don't worry about it as I know our flock is healthy.

Yield: 1½ cups

* * *

I'm always amazed at how the old-fashioned methods seem to turn me back toward Jesus. When we create a healthy culture, the good things overcome the bad; they actually take the things in front of them and transform them into something better. Let's look for every opportunity to live our lives this way—to let the bad "ferment" into something beautiful and delicious, teeming with the love of Jesus!

Chapter 4

Thrive

I have lived my entire life on the same road in the shadow of the North Cascade Range. Across the river we have a post office that is open 4 hours a day during the week. The gas station closed down a few years ago, and the nearest town is more than 10 miles away.

Most of the places are referred to by the last name of the original owner or settler of the land, not by the address. For example, one of our parcels of land on the deed is referred to as the Banner place, because that was the last name of the man from whom my grandparents purchased it. My dad's field and barn are referred to as Fruehling's, because that's the name of the old farmer he purchased it from years before I was born. You'd think after this many decades we'd refer to it by my dad's name, but that's not the way of it up here.

I remember my first overnight trip to the large, bustling city of Seattle. A friend and her sister took me out to dinner in downtown and we strolled through the streets afterward. They had both grown up in the city and were quite comfortable with the throngs of people.

We crisscrossed through traffic, and they read the streets like I could read the mountain ridges and landmarks back home. Which was a good thing, because I don't think I could have found my way from one block to the next, let alone back to where we were staying.

There was no need for a flashlight or headlamp. Store fronts, street lights, and stoplights lit up the crosswalks. I stopped in the middle of the sidewalk.

"What's the matter?" my friend asked.

I stared up at the sky. "It never gets dark here, does it?"

She followed my gaze upward. The glow from the city stretched far into the sky. "I guess it doesn't, not really."

We continued on, the soles of our shoes slapping the pavement. No worries about stepping into mud or other barnyard concerns.

My eyes kept glancing toward the sky, my subconscious working to decide if it really was nighttime or not. Trying to go to sleep with all of the lights and noise was an all-night affair. I'm used to the yip of a coyote, the serenade of frogs in the summer, and the only outside light from the wash of a full moon.

I thrive in a country environment, where "street smarts" include knowing how to tell when rain is moving down the mountain, recognizing when a storm is blowing in over the ridge, and keeping an eye out when you find bear scat around.

I'm clueless in the city, but others thrive there. They know not to ever pull out your money and feed a parking meter when you're standing by yourself and someone is eyeballing you. No matter where we find ourselves in life, be it the busy corner of a sprawling metropolis, or a quiet back pasture corner, we can thrive. We only need someone to show us the tools, the way of the land so to speak, in order to grow.

The *Merriam-Webster Dictionary* defines the word "thrive" as "to progress toward or realize a goal despite or because of circumstances."

I don't know about you, but I kind of love that this definition includes that last part of the line—"despite or because of circumstances." Because each of us have battles in our lives.

They may not be the same battle. My battlefield might be things from the past while yours is a diagnosis from the lab. But no matter what our battle may look like, each of us knows the pain and the crushingness that comes in the thick of it.

Here's the thing, though—when we have Jesus on our side, it doesn't matter what's on that battlefield. We're going to thrive. We're going to conquer that "despite" part because He conquered it when He died on the cross for our sins.

Remember when I shared about my thyroid issues? That was a battlefield for me. I felt like I was literally slogging through rubber boot–sucking mud every day for months on end.

Despite that, He led me to the point where I learned to lean on His strength because I had none of my own left. He also led me to a doctor who could help me with both prescription and natural medicines so I could thrive again.

What I love about herbal and natural medicine is we're just beginning to understand how the things God made in this world work together. While herbalism as a way of helping heal the body has been around long before the recent rise of modern medicine, we now have the science to see how or why they help with certain things.

Growing Your Own Herbs

One of my favorite things about using herbs is that you can grow many of them yourself with very little space, making them truly self-sustainable and free!

For the most part, herbs do well in small spaces and grow quite well in a container. Even my apartment- or yard-challenged friends can still grow their own herbs.

Many herbs are better suited to containers because of their invasive nature. Unless you want herbs gone wild all over your homestead (which isn't always a bad thing), you'll want to plant mint, lemon balm, oregano, and thyme in containers if you're limited in space or like a manicured garden with everything in its spot. They spread by sending out runners via their root systems, so a container helps keep them from sprawling.

But many people like to use thyme as a ground cover. It's a wonderful thing to have your landscaping be the foundations of your medicine cabinet, flavor your food, and offer such a pleasing array of foliage and flowers for the eye.

You can pick any size container—I prefer whiskey barrels that can hold multiple herbs, and smaller pots for individual herbs. Make sure there's enough room for the roots to spread out and down. If the container will be outside, make sure there are drain holes in the bottom. For large containers, fill the bottom quarter of the container with rocks to help with proper drainage and to avoid root rot, which is especially important in wetter climates like the Pacific Northwest.

Fill the rest of the way up with rich potting soil and compost. Because the dirt in the container won't receive food from surrounding soil like in regular gardens, you'll want to give it a boost of fertilizer and good compost on the top every year.

You can grow many herbs from seeds or purchase small starter plants from nurseries or plant stores. Many herbs will reseed themselves for the following year, most notably cilantro and dill.

To start seeds indoors you'll need to know your average last frost date to calculate when to begin growing your herbs from seed. You can type into Google your zip code and "first and last average frost date" if you don't know yours already.

You'll need small seed starting containers and potting soil. This is one of the few times I recommend purchasing organic potting soil. Just like human infants, baby seedlings are more susceptible to viruses and pathogens in the dirt that may be lurking in your regular garden soil. If you've ever lost seedlings before to dampening off (where baby seedlings slump over, shrivel up and die), this is probably your culprit.

You can pasteurize soil at home by heating it up in your oven, but I find it more practical to purchase it.

Pick your container. If you're reusing containers from previous plants, make sure you sterilize them by soaking them in a solution of 1 part bleach to 10 parts water for 20 minutes. Rinse and allow to dry before using.

My favorite options are to use old egg cartons (though they do tend to require a bit more watering as they're porous) or old plastic clamshell containers from store-bought produce.

Fill your container with soil, place the seeds on the surface, and wet the soil. To mimic rain and avoid the washing away of soil, I fill a spray bottle with warm water and mist my seeds. Cover with plastic to trap the moisture. This is where the clamshells come in handy, because you can simply close the lid.

Keep the soil moist, and don't allow it to dry out until your seeds have sprouted. Depending upon the seed type, this can take anywhere from 2 to 14 days. Most seeds require a soil temperature of 60° or warmer. You can use special seed-starting heat mats or place plant starts next to a heater vent or your wood stove. Check them morning and night and mist with your spray bottle to keep them moist, but not soaking wet.

Once the seeds sprout, remove the plastic covering and move to an area that has at least ten hours of light, good ventilation, and stays warm. A southern exposure window can work, but remember windows fluctuate in temperature. Seedlings shouldn't be allowed to touch the glass and should be taken away from the window at night when temperatures dip.

If your seedlings get leggy and are reaching toward the window, they're not getting adequate light. You can try rotating the trays but your best bet is to use a grow light.

My grow light is small and I set it up in a corner of the living room. I prefer a grow light that allows you to move the light so as your seedlings grow you can raise the light with them. Keep the light about an inch from the top of the plants and raise it as the plants grow. This helps produce stronger stems, as they're not reaching toward the light.

The second biggest mistake people make when growing their own seedlings, next to not sterilizing, is not exposing their seedlings to movement. Outdoors they have the rain hitting their leaves and the wind moving their stems. This results in a stronger plant.

Seedlings indoors are wimps. They need the stimuli to become strong. It reminds me of the adversities and hard times in my own life, because these are always the times when I do the most growing and my faith gets a super shot of maturity.

An easy way to mimic the outdoors for your seedlings is to to gently run your hand over the top of the plants whenever you walk by. You could put a small fan on them, but I'd rather not have to use any more electricity than necessary.

When you're ready to transplant your seedlings outdoors, make sure you harden them off. This is a process of taking them outdoors for longer periods of time each day over a week before planting them in their permanent spot. If you don't take this step, you'll end up putting your seedlings into shock and most likely killing them.

Find a spot that is sheltered from hard winds and doesn't get too hot. Put your seedlings outdoors for 1 hour the first day. Increase their time outdoors by 2 hours each day over a week.

When transplanting, dig a hole twice as wide if possible but the same depth as the container the plant is in. If the roots are bound together, take the edge of your spade and gently break them up so they can easily spread out and find food for the plant. Fill in the hole with soil and make sure the soil is at the same line on the stem as it was in the container (an exception to this is tomatoes, which need be planted deeper than their seedling pot level) Water well.

You can keep some herbs in the house as long as they get adequate sunlight or are under a grow light. Many folks will bring in their basil or other tender herbs so they can harvest them all year long. Never fear, no matter how cold your climate is, you can have year-round herbs via a windowsill herb garden. And are you ready for this? You can grow basil without any dirt! I've successfully grown basil indoors through the winter in just water!

Step 1: Have you ever been at the grocery store and seen those little packages of living basil? Buy one or two bunches (usually about three plants are inside each package). Growing basil in water during the winter months is actually preferable, as you don't have to worry about your soil molding.

Step 2: Choose a planter. You'll need a planter of some kind and the most frugal option is to use something you already have at home. I have a thing for Mason jars, especially the vintage blue ones. Make sure your jar is washed and rinsed well. The quart size work best as they're taller and offer more support for the basil.

Step 3: Add water. Put about an inch of water in the bottom of your jar. (Note: If you're on city water or have chlorine in your water, you'll need to use untreated water.) You don't have to add liquid silica, but because silica is normally found in soil, the addition of it will help the cell structure of your plant. It's available at most nurseries and plant stores. It comes very concentrated, so just a drop is all you'll need in each jar.

Step 4: Place your basil plants in the water. Find the warmest and sunniest window in your home, which is usually a southern exposure side of the house. Because your plants have been inside a store with very little sunlight, don't be alarmed if the leaves seem wilted and shriveled the first few days. Place the plant in the window and wait a week. All but one of mine perked up after some TLC in the sunlight.

Be sure you don't place the basil against the glass or allow the leaves to touch it. The glass will be quite a bit cooler than the air and can kill the plant, especially during nighttime temps. If an exceptionally cold night is in the forecast, you should move your plants out of the windowsill onto the counter where it's warmer overnight.

Replace the water every week or two.

Once your basil is doing well in its new home, you'll want to harvest it. Now, harvesting basil isn't hard, but here are a few tips to ensure the continued growth of your herbs. Contrary to what you'd think, leave the large bottom leaves of basil on the bottom alone. These are what feed your plant.

When you've got pairs of leaves at the top of your plant in a few tiers, pinch off leaves directly above a pair. This will cause two new shoots to grow, creating more leaves, and a bushier, stronger plant.

Favorite Perennial Herbs

Some herbs are perennials and will come back every year. These are some of my favorites, as they require only planting once and not as much care. If your area gets extremely cold, some perennial herbs may act as annuals, meaning you'll have to replant them each spring if you don't cover them up or bring them inside during the cold months.

Some herbs are annuals, but due to their self-seeding nature, they act as a perennial and you generally don't have to replant them manually each year.

Knowing the microclimates on your property and yard is key. For example, rosemary doesn't generally overwinter well in my area. However, I've had one plant in a large dark-colored container right next to our back deck in southern exposure—the warmest part of our homestead—winter over for 4 years straight without doing a thing to it. But I've had rosemary in other locations on our land and it didn't make it through winter.

- Chamomile—there are two types of chamomile: Roman Chamomile is a perennial, whereas German Chamomile is an annual, but it tends to self-seed, so it acts as a perennial. German Chamomile has more studies done on it and is generally used more overall than Roman Chamomile.

- Chives—excellent as a container herb or planted directly in the ground. It will spread out, so when the plant gets too big, simply take a sharp, pointed shovel and divide it out. It will die back during the winter and send up new shoots in the spring.

- Comfrey—has a long root system, making it very tolerable to both hot and cold weather. It is often planted under fruit trees. Just be aware that the plant is almost impossible to eradicate or remove once it's established. It produces pretty purple and violet blossoms.

- Echinacea—also called coneflower, has beautiful blooms and will come back year after year. Echinacea makes a pretty bouquet as well. It prefers full sun, but will tolerate some shade.

- Lavender—a beautiful addition to your landscaping and flower beds. It prefers full sun and well-draining soil, doesn't like to have its roots wet, and does well in raised beds or rock gardens. In the early spring, trim back the plant to a few inches tall.

- Rosemary—does best in full sun with well-draining soil,

but will tolerate some shade. Some varieties are more cold tolerant than others.

- Oregano—prefers full sun, but if your area gets really hot, afternoon shade won't bother it. It tends to spread, so either keep it trimmed (helps create a bushier plant) or plant in an area where you don't mind if it spreads out.

- Sage—likes a good amount of sun, but tolerates afternoon shade. It's a gorgeous addition to landscaping because its leaves are a beautiful silver green and quite soft to the touch. It does well in containers or the garden ground. It's fairly hardy, and I can harvest fresh leaves well into December in our Zone 7.

- Thyme—also likes full sun and holds up well to drought or low water. I like a low-maintenance plant, and thyme fits the bill nicely. It also will make a home in either a container or the garden.

Annual Herb Seed Starting Chart

Herb	Days to Germinate	Weeks to Start Before Last Frost	When to Plant Outdoors	When to Direct Sow
Basil	5 to 10 Days	4 to 8 weeks	2 to 3 weeks after last frost, can stagger plant all summer	2 to 4 weeks after last frost
Calendula	5 to 15 days	6 to 8 weeks	1 to 2 weeks after last frost	After last frost

German Chamomile	7 to 14 days	4 to 8 weeks	1 week after last frost	2 to 4 weeks before last frost
Cilantro/ Coriander	5 to 10 days	4 to 8 weeks	Right at last frost	2 weeks before last frost
Dill	10 to 14 days	It does better direct sown		4 weeks after last frost or when soil temperature is 60 to 70°
Summer Savory	2 to 3 weeks	6 to 8 weeks	After danger of last frost has passed	1 week after average last frost date

How to Harvest Herbs

To keep most herbs from getting leggy, you'll want to pinch off the leaves from the top of the plant, not the bottom. This can be done as needed for cooking or when the plant begins to get too big.

I use my hands if I'm just collecting a few leaves for a recipe. But if harvesting a larger amount, a sharp pair of scissors or gardening shears are best. Remember, we don't want to crush or bruise the leaves before use. We want all that flavor in our food.

How to Dry Your Own Herbs

Pick herbs in the morning, right after the dew is gone. They have the highest concentration of oils in their leaves at this time of day. Basil is the exception and can be picked a bit later in the morning.

Lightly rinse your herbs to remove any dust or other unseen debris. I'm sure you practice organic gardening at home, so we don't have to worry about any icky chemicals or pesticides. Place herbs on an absorbent towel to suck up the rinse water.

Be careful not to crush or bruise your herbs before drying. You'll lose the oils if this happens and that is where the flavors are concentrated. If possible, dry herbs on the stalk and remove the leaves after they're dry for storing.

There are two ways to dry herbs: a dehydrator or the old-fashioned hanging method. If the weather is damp or has high humidity, you may want to go with the dehydrator method.

- Old-fashioned method. Tie the ends of no more than four to five stalks of herbs together. Hang the bunches upside down in a warm dry area, out of direct sunlight. Allow to dry until leaves crumble at your touch. Depending upon the moisture content in your leaves and the climate, this can take anywhere from a week to a month. Check periodically for any mildew or mold growth. Discard if mold or mildew are present. We tried putting our herbs in a pillowcase and hanging it to keep dust away, but there wasn't enough air flow and they ended up molding.

- Dehydrator method. Place your herbs in a single layer on your dehydrator tray, making sure they're not touching. Because the herbs will shrink dramatically when dried, I use my fruit leather screens. You want to make sure there's enough room between the herbs for the air to circulate. Dehydrate your herbs at 95°, which is the lowest possible setting on my dehydrator. Check them at 12 hours. One year, we had excessive rain, and it took 24 hours for my herbs to dry. Because herbs don't seem to transfer flavors when drying, you can dry them together. I've had four trays going at once with chocolate mint, spearmint, oregano, basil, and thyme.

Once herbs are dry, crumble them with your fingers into clean dry jars. I prefer glass jars, as plastic containers seem to affect the flavor of the herbs over time.

Common Herbs

	Culinary Use	Medicinal Use
Arnica	Do not take by mouth or internally, as this can cause serious side effects.[1]	This has been used for centuries in topical salves for aiding bruises, sprains, and sore muscles. You'll find it in many topical gels or ointments even on store shelves.
Basil	Basil is one of the most popular flavorings in Italian dishes and is great when used in soups, dressings, and salads. Especially a favorite paired with sliced tomatoes and mozzarella cheese.	Basil is used to help aid digestion and also has antibacterial properties.
Calendula	Calendula can be used in tea and has been used to color butter and cheeses.	This is a wonderful herb for the skin and basically an all-around work horse. It has anti-inflammatory and antiseptic properties, which makes it a great candidate for multiple skin issues and also for wound care. It smells wonderful, and also has history as a dye due to its orange blossom. Because calendula is considered a gentle herb, you'll find it in a lot of natural products for children. (Always check before using any herb or essential oils on children.)

Cardamom	This is a strong spice, so a little goes a long way. It's often paired in fruit desserts or custards, similar to cinnamon, and is a highlight in many Indian dishes.	Cardamom can be used as a digestive aid.
Cayenne	Cayenne adds heat to any dish and is commonly used in Mexican recipes.	You'll find this spice in pain relief creams on the pharmacy store shelf as capsaicin cream, used to help aid the relief of muscle, nerve and joint pain. Never apply to open wounds or skin to avoid burning the skin or causing blisters. Use a small amount and lower strength when first using topically. As a medicinal spice it helps aid digestion, is thought to help boost the metabolism, and might help prevent blood clotting. Caution: Don't use prior to surgical procedures, if you're on blood thinning medications, or if you have a blood clotting disorder.

Chamomile	This herb is commonly used to make a soothing tea.	This little white flower plant is another common garden plant. It's been around for centuries and is used to support feelings of calmness and to aid nervous stomachs. Many people enjoy chamomile as a bedtime tea. Chamomile is often used in wound care to help promote healing. Recent studies show it can help improve cardiovascular conditions and support immune systems.[2]
Chili Powder	Chili powder is used in almost every Mexican dish and often added to other dishes for flavor. It's the base of many homemade spice mixes.	See *Cayenne*. Make sure your chili powder doesn't contain any other additives before using.
Chives	Chives are one of our favorite herbs to add to potatoes, eggs, casseroles, salads, meats, and soups. They're a member of the allium (onion family) and are delicious both fresh and dried.	Chives are used to help aid digestion and also contain vitamins C and A.
Cinnamon	Cinnamon is used in a variety of baked goods. It pairs well with fruit and pumpkin. I've even used it to flavor some stews or chili. It's a warm spice and is probably one of the most used in many a pantry.	Medicinally, cinnamon is a powerful little spice. It's used to help aid digestion and also has antiviral and antifungal properties. Cassia cinnamon has large amounts of the compound coumarin and can harm the liver in large doses.[3]

Comfrey	Comfrey should not be taken internally without the recommendation of a medical professional.	A common medicinal plant, often known as bone-knit. Comfrey also contains a chemical called pyrrolizidine alkaloids that can damage the liver and lungs and is not advised for internal use.[4]
Coriander	Coriander is the seeds from cilantro. The leaves of cilantro are used mainly fresh for flavoring salsas and pico de gallo. The seed is used mainly in Mexican dishes after it's ground up, but also is used in Indian curry dishes.	Coriander is used to help aid digestion, and studies have found it effective in killing some parasites.[5]
Cumin	Cumin is traditional in many Mexican and Indian dishes.	Cumin has been proven to help boost the immune system[6] as well as having many antioxidant properties.
Curry	Curry is found in many Indian recipes and cuisine. It's actually a blend of many spices together, with turmeric as the base. Usually it includes cumin, turmeric, coriander, black pepper, fenugreek, red pepper, ginger, celery, and cardamom.	Curry may help reduce inflammation, aids digestion, and may help blood sugar levels.

Dandelion	Dandelions send down a long taproot, making them hard to eradicate from your yard, but excellent come harvest time. Pull the plant up by the root, rinse off the dirt, and dehydrate for storage. In the spring when the leaves are young, you can add it to salads or any other dish as salad green. The blossoms can be dipped in batter and fried. The roots are a powerhouse as well.	Dandelion is thought to aid with digestion, has traditionally been used in the past for liver issues, and as a diuretic.[7]
Echinacea	This herb is commonly used to make a soothing tea.	This is one of the herbs I use frequently once my kids start back to school and cough and cold season go into overdrive. Echinacea is used for its ability to help support the immune system.
Garlic	Garlic is used daily in our home. In fact, we grow about 70 bulbs of garlic every year and we're of the opinion that if a recipe calls for garlic, always double or triple the amount.	Medicinally, garlic may cover the widest range of ailments. Garlic contains a chemical called allicin. It is used to treat many conditions related to the heart and blood system, including blood pressure and cholesterol, cancer, bacterial and viral infections, topically to the skin, common cold symptoms, and stomach ailments.[8]

Ginger	Ginger is a main spice in baking, especially ginger-bread, apple, and pumpkin recipes. A little goes a long way, as it can have a bit of a kick to it.	Ginger is thought to help all sorts of stomach ailments, including nausea and vomiting, pain, and inflammation, and it also has antibacterial properties as well as immune support.[9] This is also one that you shouldn't use if you're on blood thinning medications or have blood clotting disorders.
Lavender	The blossoms should be harvested before they begin to dry out, or when they first start to open. They can be added to teas or used in baking.	Lavender is probably the most commonly used herb for its calming and soothing properties. I put a drop of lavender essential oil on my pillow every night when I go to bed. I also make lavender sachets for my husband's truck and keep dried bunches of it around the house. Lavender works well to help soothe the skin and is often used in preparations for burn relief and pain. The blossoms can be infused into oil for salves and creams.
Marjoram	Related to oregano, marjoram is commonly used in savory dishes.	Marjoram has antiseptic, antibacterial, and antiviral properties. It also helps aid digestion and has been shown to help decrease the occurrence of stomach ulcers and acid.[10] It has also shown promise in helping women with polycystic ovary syndrome[11].

Marshmallow Root	Used to flavor candies.	Marshmallow root can help soothe a sore throat and ease the swelling and pain of mucus membranes in the respiratory tract.[12]
Mustard	Mustard is commonly used in many of our pickling brines and condiments, especially mustard for sandwiches and added in powdered form to homemade barbecue sauces.	Mustard is surprisingly strong in antioxidants and is antibacterial. So much so, that research shows mustard can help fight and may prevent certain types of cancer.[13] Mustard is a long time standby for helping aid respiratory symptoms.
Nutmeg	Nutmeg is another favorite spice when it comes to baking. It completes my trinity of baking spices with cinnamon and ginger.	Nutmeg is thought to help aid digestion symptoms and to contain some antibacterial and antifungal properties.[14]
Oregano	Oregano is the base for many Mexican and Italian dishes. It pairs well with tomato-based recipes, beef, and chicken.	Oregano is used to help aid the digestion system, possibly help reduce cough, and has antifungal, antibacterial, and antiviral properties. It also helps eliminate parasites.

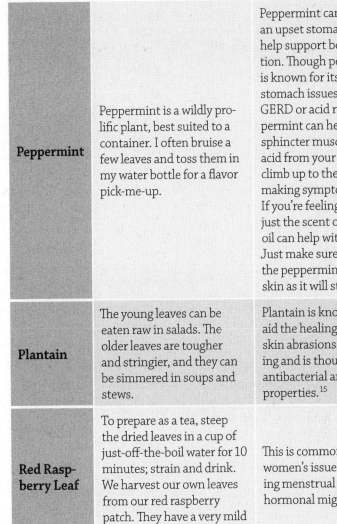

Peppermint	Peppermint is a wildly prolific plant, best suited to a container. I often bruise a few leaves and toss them in my water bottle for a flavor pick-me-up.	Peppermint can soothe an upset stomach and help support bowel function. Though peppermint is known for its use with stomach issues, if you have GERD or acid reflux, peppermint can help relax the sphincter muscle, allowing acid from your stomach to climb up to the esophagus, making symptoms worse. If you're feeling congested, just the scent of peppermint oil can help with congestion. Just make sure you don't get the peppermint oil on your skin as it will sting and burn.
Plantain	The young leaves can be eaten raw in salads. The older leaves are tougher and stringier, and they can be simmered in soups and stews.	Plantain is known to help aid the healing of wounds, skin abrasions, and swelling and is thought to have antibacterial and antifungal properties.[15]
Red Raspberry Leaf	To prepare as a tea, steep the dried leaves in a cup of just-off-the-boil water for 10 minutes; strain and drink. We harvest our own leaves from our red raspberry patch. They have a very mild flavor.	This is commonly used for women's issues, from relieving menstrual cramps to hormonal migraines.

Rosemary	Rosemary is a particularly fragrant herb. I rarely roast a whole chicken or turkey without the use of rosemary. I pluck a couple of fresh stalks and put them in the cavity of the bird. Whenever I'm making broth or stock, rosemary goes into the mix. It's rare I make a soup that a bit of rosemary doesn't jump in the pot as well. Rosemary pairs well with just about every type of red meat.	Rosemary is commonly used for digestion issues, hair loss, and has anti-inflammatory and analgesic properties.
Sage	This silvery-green leaf herb is one of my favorites because it's easy to grow, lasts almost a year in my garden, and is just so tasty. I use sage with my meat balls, meatloaf, and many a soup and broth.	Sage is used to support digestive problems and supports mind and mental performance.[16] It can decrease milk when nursing, so a sage tea can be soothing when weaning. Of course, it's not recommended to use any herb medicinally when breastfeeding without first checking with your medical professional. Sage helps decrease secretions and extra mucus and is often used to help aid sore mouth, throat, and swollen nasal passages.

Stinging Nettle	In the spring when the leaves are young, they can be added to soups and stews or sautéed in butter and garlic as a side dish. Once they're cooked the leaves no longer sting, so no worries. Make sure you wear gloves and long-sleeved shirts when harvesting. They really do live up to their name.	Stinging nettles are thought to help with decreasing inflammation and urine output.[17]
Thyme	Thyme is used as a flavoring in many dishes, especially Italian.	Thyme supports the immune system during cough and cold season. It can also help soothe a sore throat.
Turmeric	This spice is typically found in Indian and Asian dishes and is known for its bright yellow color.	Turmeric is a wonderful addition to add to your chicken soup as it helps boost the immune system, and is now becoming more widely known for its antioxidant and anti-inflammatory properties. However, it can be harder for the body to put that turmeric to work and absorb it unless you eat it with fat or black pepper.[18]

Culinary Uses of Herbs

Now let's put those spices to use. If you're using fresh herbs in a recipe that calls for dried herbs, you'll need to use three times the amount of fresh herbs the recipe calls for.

If you've ever plunked down money for those little seasoning mix packets at the store or not been able to make a recipe because you didn't have one of those little packets, then this section is just for you. Many of those seasoning packets contain anticaking agents and ingredients made from GMO crops in the form of both corn and soy, just to name a few reasons I don't buy them. Plus, when one is making them at home, one can customize the flavor to their tastes, grow a good portion of the ingredients themselves, and save a ton of money by making their own. Whew, that's a whole lot of reasons to love these recipes.

Feel free to double or triple these recipes, but remember, when we're mixing spices and herbs, it's best to keep them to smaller batches (I wouldn't do a quart size jar) at a time so you use it up before it starts caking. While the shelf life of spices and herbs is quite long—one to two years if they're kept dry and away from heat and light—the best flavor will be within six months of mixing. If they start to clump up (remember, there is no silicone dioxide or other anticaking agents in these babies), simply take the end of a spoon and break up the largest clumps and stir. Make sure you're not storing them right above your stove where heat and moisture will contribute to faster caking.

Thoroughly combine all the ingredients together in a bowl first to ensure even mixing (or shake really well in the jar if there's enough room). Spoon the mixed blend into your container of choice. Whenever I'm pouring anything I use a funnel if possible. Put a lid on it and label your jar. That's it—you're set to go.

Taco Seasoning

  ¼ cup chili powder
  2 T. cumin
  1 T. onion powder
  1 T. garlic powder
  1 tsp. dried oregano
  2 tsp. paprika
  1 T. salt

2 tsp. ground black pepper

½ tsp. crushed red pepper flakes (or to taste)

Combine all the ingredients into a glass jar. When making tacos, brown 1 pound of ground beef (or cubed chicken), drain off fat, stir in ½ cup water and 2 tablespoons of taco seasoning, or to taste. Stir well, until all the meat is coated, and allow to simmer for 1 to 2 minutes.

Chili Seasoning

¼ cup chili powder

¼ cup cumin powder

2½ T. onion powder

2½ T. garlic powder

1½ T. paprika

1½ T. dried oregano

2 T. sea salt

1 tsp. ground black pepper

1 tsp. crushed red pepper flakes (or to taste)

Combine all ingredients in a glass jar. Use 4 tablespoons of the mix to one pot of chili. The above recipe is what I use in our 4½-quart slow cooker.

Italian Seasoning

¼ cup basil

2 T. oregano

2 T. thyme

2 T. marjoram

2 T. rosemary

1 T. sage
1 tsp. garlic granules (optional)

Mix all ingredients together in a bowl and transfer to your container. Use this to taste in spaghetti sauce, pizza, stew, soups (especially tomato), or even sprinkle on butter when making garlic bread.

Ranch Dressing

2 T. dried parsley
5 tsp. dill weed
1 T. chives
1 T. onion powder
1 T. garlic powder
1 tsp. salt
½ tsp. basil
¼ tsp. ground black pepper

Mix all of the ingredients together and place in a glass jar.

For ranch dip: Use 2 tablespoons (or to taste) of the mix with 2 tablespoons of mayo and ¾ cup yogurt (or sour cream).

For ranch dressing: Use 1 tablespoon with ⅓ cup mayonnaise and ⅓ cup buttermilk (for a traditional flavor) or sub in ⅓ cup regular milk. You can add more mayo to make it thicker or more milk for a runnier dressing.

Add a tablespoon of dry mix to your popcorn for homemade ranch popcorn, but be warned, it's slightly addictive.

Popcorn Seasoning

1 T. nutritional yeast
½ T. powdered cheddar cheese, optional
1 to 2 tsp. sea salt

½ **T. garlic powder**
Dash of paprika or chili power

Sprinkle onto popcorn to desired taste (melted butter drizzled on the popcorn first is a must at our house).

Basil Pesto

Add garlic to taste in this recipe. The amount you use will depend on the size of your cloves—I always think more is better! The pine nuts are a traditional pesto ingredient, but since they add so much to the cost I rarely include them.

2 cups fresh basil leaves
2 to 6 cloves peeled garlic
Pinch of sea salt
¾ to 1 cup olive oil
½ cup freshly grated Parmesan cheese
¼ cup pine nuts (optional)

Place all the ingredients in a high-powered blender or food processor and process until smooth and well blended together. Start with the smaller amount of olive oil and add more if needed to blend well.

Cover tightly and store in the fridge or freeze. Many people like to freeze pesto in an ice cube tray—once frozen, pop out the cubes of pesto and keep in a freezer container to add to sauces when cooking. My friend Julie puts her pesto in a gallon freezer bag and lays it flat to freeze in a thin single layer, and then breaks off however much she needs when cooking.

Yield: 1¼ cups

Medicinal Uses of Herbs

Many herbs will already be "hiding" in your regular seasonings in your pantry, but some will have strictly medicinal purposes only. Please, do your research and confirm with your medical professionals before using herbs medicinally as they can counteract other medicines you may be taking.

Now, I need to be up front and honest with you here. I am not an herbalist. I'm not a medical doctor, and nothing I'm about to share with you should be taken as a diagnosis or treatment of any kind. Before using any herbal product, you truly should consult with your doctor and pharmacist for dosing, interactions with current medications or conditions, and safety.

There's a bit of misconception with folks that because something is natural it's safe. That is not true, my friends. Many herbs and natural spices have true effects on the body and can interact with certain medications or medical conditions.

For example, my daughter has a blood clotting disorder—Von Willebrand disease, to be exact. She must stay away from ginger, so no ginger honey or even candied ginger for her.

While I don't want to scare you away from using herbs, I do want you to be responsible and use good judgment. I believe we're blessed to live in a day and age where we have the benefit of both modern and traditional medicines.

Growing up, I rarely went to the doctor. We didn't have insurance, and unless you were really sick, you toughed it out. Luckily, I didn't have many illnesses or need of the doctor often.

After going through GERD and stomach acid issues, including an endoscope and biopsy of my upper stomach and esophagus, I discovered that my healing came from changing my diet and the things we used in our home.

It sparked our journey to *The Made-from-Scratch Life*, and seeking out alternative and natural ways in both our health and home. Herbs weren't something we used in my home growing up, except for occasional culinary purposes.

On my own, I began diving into natural medicine and herbal uses. What I'm sharing with you are things I've learned on my journey and the things we use in our home.

In case you haven't noticed, I'm kind of fascinated by the old way of doing things. While having a special fondness for the pioneers during the American Old West days due to the Laura Ingalls Wilder books, my appreciation goes back much further.

When we look at the ancient cities and the way people lived before our modern conveniences, I'm humbled at how good we have it now. Most of us aren't hiking outside to find clean water or even to an outdoor well to heave on a rope to get a bucket of water (at least in first-world countries and most of Western civilization). We flip a little lever on our faucet and both hot and cold water come rushing into our homes.

Can you imagine being able to treat someone only with various roots and leaves? In modern society, what a typical mother or wife knows about using medicinal plants in her area is virtually forgotten. It wasn't passed down in my family, and it may not have been in yours, either.

While I firmly believe in using modern medicine (it saved my life when I had an ectopic pregnancy) and think it can be a wonderful gift God has given us, I also believe in using the natural plants He created. After all, God is the master herbalist, He made them all.

The first place we look to for herb use is in our pantry cupboard. Most of us have a few (or not so few) bottles of dried herbs we use to tasty up a dish. Did you know that many of those herbs not only serve to make our food taste better, but often times, those tasty bits actually have beneficial medicinal properties as well?

While much of modern Western medicine doesn't use herbs in general medical practice, Germany uses herbs in their regular medicine with their German Commission E, a scientific advisory board that evaluates the safety and efficacy of the herbs used for licensed medical practitioners in Germany. Your regular doctor may or may not recommend herbs, but licensed naturopaths will. I strongly recommend talking with your doctor, pharmacist, and naturopath before beginning the use of any herbs medicinally.

For those of you wishing to further your studies, I highly recommend Rosemary Gladstar's *Medicinal Herbs: A Beginner's Guide: 33 Healing Herbs to Know, Grow, and Use* and *Alchemy of Herbs:*

Transform Everyday Ingredients into Foods and Remedies That Heal by Rosalee de la Forêt.

These resources are used by many experienced herbalists.

Herbal Tea Infusions

As you step into the world of herbs you'll likely hear terminology thrown around. The first and easiest form is one most of us are familiar with and that is tea, also referred to as an infusion. We're infusing water with the essence of the herbs. Infusions and teas are best suited to the leaves and flowers of a plant.

Choose your herb or herbs of choice to make your tea or infusion. If you have a tea ball or empty tea bags, fill them with your herbs (usually 1 to 2 teaspoons worth) and bring water to a boil. Pour just-off-the-boil water on top of the herbs and allow to steep for at least 5 minutes or up to 15 minutes. The longer it steeps, the stronger it will be. Strain out herbs, add any sweetener if using such as honey, and sip.

When I have a cold coming, I make this tea to help aid my sore throat and relieve my stuffed up nose.

> 1½ tsp. fresh sage leaves (or ¾ teaspoon dried)
> ¾ tsp. marshmallow leaf
> 2 tsp. raw honey

Place herbs in a tea bag or tea ball. Pour just-off-the-boil water into your cup and allow to seep for 10 minutes. Remove the herbs and stir in the honey. Sip and enjoy!

Note: Never give raw honey to children under 1 year of age due to the risk of botulism.

Decoctions

This method takes longer but is similar to making a tea or infusion. This is usually the choice when using the roots, bark, or seeds of the plant.

Place your pieces of herbs into the bottom of a small saucepan, usually about 2 tablespoons worth. Cover with two to four cups of water.

Bring to a gentle boil over medium-low heat. Allow to simmer for 15 to 30 minutes then strain, allow to cool to a safe sipping temperature, and drink.

Note: You can still use the roots or bark when making an infusion or tea; it just won't be as strong as a decoction. I often make tea blends with both leaves and roots or bark.

Herbal Tinctures

While *tincture* sounds very official, it's really the same thing as making our own extracts. To get started, you'll need a clean glass jar, herbs, and alcohol.

Let's chat a minute about the alcohol. There can be strong feelings about the use of alcohol. In the case of tinctures or extract, it helps preserve the herbs and give a long shelf life. It's also the vehicle that extracts the good properties from the herb. Most times, only a small amount of the tincture is used at a time, and when added to a hot beverage, the heat evaporates the alcohol, leaving the herb behind. Alcohol is needed because its strong solvency helps extract some herbs, especially those made from the bark or roots. *(If you're uncomfortable using alcohol, keep reading for instructions on making vinegar- and glycerin-based tinctures.)* What's the best alcohol to use?

- Some people prefer to use vodka because it is clear and relatively tasteless. If you're concerned about GMOs or gluten, because most commercially made vodka is made from grains (although some specialty ones are made from potatoes and even grapes), then search out a local organic brand. Make sure your alcohol is 80 to 100 proof.

- Rum is made from the byproducts of molasses or sugar cane, which means there aren't any GMO crops involved. Due to the fermentation process to make rum, there's basically not any sugar left either. I use rum for my tinctures and extracts as I don't have a local source for purchasing organic vodka.

Finely chop your desired herbs. It is usually best to make your tinctures with just one herb, and then mix it with other tinctures if desired upon use.

One of the benefits of making an herbal tincture is you can use fresh plant material. It doesn't have to be dried, though you can use dried herbs as well. You want to chop or grind up the herbs in order to release the oils more easily.

Fill a clean glass jar with your herbs, but remember that dried herbs will swell up as they reconstitute, so don't fill the jar as full. For dried herbs, fill your container about a quarter of the way full; if using fresh herbs, halfway full, for a good rule of thumb.

Pour the alcohol, vinegar, or glycerin over the herbs by at least 2 to 3 inches. Cover the jar and shake well. Set it in a warm area (heat helps with the extraction) for 6 weeks, shaking daily if you remember.

Make sure to check on your tincture and add more liquid if needed to keep the herbs covered by 2 to 3 inches.

After six weeks, line a colander or sieve with cheesecloth and place it over a glass bowl (I always use my large Pyrex mixing bowl with the handle and pour spout) and pour the mixture through it.

Pour the strained tincture into a clean glass container with a tight-fitting lid. Light is the enemy so many people will use dark blue or dark amber glass bottles with dropper lids. You can also use a clean Mason jar. Just make sure you store it away from light.

Label your container with the type of tincture (herb used) and the date it was made. Maybe you're like me and think there's no way you'll forget what is in a jar, but time has a way of stealing that knowledge. Put a label on it.

Vinegar Tinctures

Follow the above instructions but use vinegar instead of the alcohol. In her book *Medicinal Herbs: A Beginner's Guide*, Rosemary Gladstar recommends warming the vinegar before using to help release the herbal constituents. Raw apple cider vinegar is commonly used as a natural health tonic, and as long as you just warm it, you won't destroy any of the good stuff and will add more goodness to your tincture.

Glycerin Tinctures

If you don't want to use alcohol or vinegar, you can make tinctures with glycerin. Make sure you always use a food-grade glycerin, which is made from vegetable oils and is naturally sweet. Some glycerin is only for external or body care use.

You also need to dilute your glycerin with distilled water before pouring over your herbs. It's best to use distilled water so you don't introduce contaminants. Use 3 parts glycerin to 1 part distilled water. Store in refrigerator for up to one year.

The Best Liquid for Your Tinctures

This depends on a few factors. The strongest and longest lasting medicinal tincture is an alcohol-based one (make sure you use 80 to 100 proof). Assuming you're storing it in a cool spot away from the light, this can last four years or longer.

Vinegar tinctures can be used in your cooking, and because they use raw apple cider vinegar, you can make your own solvent (the vinegar) and grow the herbs at home, making this a free and self-sustainable route. A vinegar tincture will last for one year.

Glycerin tinctures still have medicinal properties, though not as strong as the first two, but this makes them a better candidate for using with children or people who cannot have alcohol. It's naturally sweet, which benefits picky palates. It will last you two to three years.

I have used all three depending on the herb, who will be using it, and the supplies I have on hand.

How to Use Herbal Tinctures

Herbal tinctures can be taken straight, but due to their potency, most herbalists recommend you dilute them in tea, water, or juice.

Tinctures are generally measured by dropperfuls (the little glass droppers with the rubber bulb on the end) or a teaspoonful, depending upon the herb used in the tincture and the form.

Please review the herb, use, and dosage before using your tinctures medicinally. Visit the Resource page at http://handmadethebook.com/ where you can find more in-depth information.

Herb-Infused Oil

Making an herb oil is an excellent way to infuse your homemade salves and balms with extra medicinal properties. I make several different kinds of herbal oils to have on hand.

I've found the best containers are Mason jars, but any glass container with a lid will do. Fill a quart-sized (4 cup volume) Mason jar with approximately ¾ to 1 cup dried leaves or blossoms. Cover the herbs by 1 inch with extra virgin olive oil (avocado or jojoba oil can be used as well). Make sure you leave a ½ inch headspace, because the dried herbs absorb the oil and expand.

Place a lid on and shake well. Set the jar in a sunny, warm window.

Shake the jar once a day to help infuse the oil. If the oil level drops below the herbs, add more oil until they're completely submerged.

After 4 to 6 weeks, strain the oil through cheesecloth or a fine-mesh sieve. Store your herb-infused oil in a glass bottle in a dark and cool place, making sure you label it with the type of herbs and the date made. The oil should last for up to a year. You can add a few drops of vitamin E oil to help prolong the shelf life.

Note: It's always best to used dried herbs and plants rather than fresh to avoid moisture and bacteria growth in your infused oil.

Fast Herb-Infused Oil

Am I the only one who doesn't always plan ahead? Sometimes we need a way to do something that doesn't take 4 to 6 weeks. This is the method you can use to make herb-infused oil in just a day. You'll just need a slow cooker or a double boiler.

Measure out the herbs into a glass Mason jar. Cover the herbs by 2 inches with oil. Place the Mason jar into your slow cooker, filled with about 2 inches of water. (You can also place the Mason jar in a saucepan with water on low heat as a double boiler.) The goal is to have the warm water surround the jar, effectively heating the oil to draw the properties from the herbs into the oil. Bring up to a low heat, preferably between 95° to 120°. We want as many of the medicinal properties to remain in the herbs as possible.

Allow to infuse until the oil has taken on the scent and color of the herbs, preferably for 2 to 8 hours, but the longer the better provided the heat is low. Even on low my slow cooker tends to get pretty hot, so using a cooking thermometer to test the temperature periodically is a great idea. Keep the lid off when using your slow cooker to keep the temperature lower. I actually found that the "keep warm" setting worked best on my model to keep temps right around 100°.

When the oil is finished infusing, take it off the heat and allow it to cool. Strain the oil through cheesecloth. Store your herb-infused oil in a glass bottle in a dark and cool place, making sure you label it with the type of herbs and the date made. The oil should last for up to a year. You can add a few drops of vitamin E oil to help prolong the shelf life.

Lip Balm

Using your infused herbal oil in this recipe will give it another scent boost as well as medicinal properties. Some of my top choices of infused oils for lip balm are peppermint, calendula, or lavender.

When making homemade salves, lotions, and balms, it really is best to get a small food scale so you can measure your ingredients by weight instead of volume to be accurate. However, lip balm is a smaller recipe, so you can usually get away with measuring instead of weighing.

The cocoa butter gives this a nice smell and pairs nicely with spearmint or orange essential oil. Please make sure you use an essential oil and brand that is safe for external use before ever adding it to your products.

> **1 T. infused avocado oil (0.45 ounces by weight)**
> **1 T. cocoa butter (0.45 ounces by weight)**
> **1 T. beeswax (0.45 ounces by weight)**
> **8 to 10 drops essential oil (optional)**

Using a double boiler, or a small saucepan with a large Pyrex measuring bowl on top, heat the first three ingredients on medium-low heat, stirring frequently. When everything is liquefied, remove from heat and stir in essential oils if using. Immediately begin filling your containers, because the balm will start to cool and solidify rather quickly.

Fill lip balm containers ¾ of the way full and allow to slightly cool. This takes only a minute or two and prevents a tunnel or hole forming in the top of your lip balm. Once the balm has cooled (it will start to harden and lighten in color), fill to the top of the container. Allow to cool, place lid on, and use. I keep the pot simmering so I can set the balm back on if it starts to cool too much before topping them off.

A glass eyedropper is very helpful in filling the containers. I keep a dedicated one for making balm as it's pretty much impossible to clean it out thoroughly. If the balm hardens inside the dropper, let it simmer in the water for a few minutes, expel the liquid, and dry before the next use. (You never want to introduce any water into your lip balm as this can encourage bacteria growth.)

If you use the pouring method, some of the lip balm will harden along the spout and side of the glass. Hold the Pyrex on its side above the steam of the double broiler until the balm is melted to get every last drop—be careful, it's hot and steamy. Immediately pour into your last container.

To test the consistency of the lip balm, place a saucer or small bowl in the freezer before making. When the ingredients are fully melted, take a small amount and place it on the cold saucer or plate. It will harden very fast. Rub it on your lips to test.

Add a small amount more oil if it's too firm. If it's too soft, add a small amount of beeswax. Test again until it's reached your desired state. It's much easier to make adjustments this way, because once it's in the tubes, you're kind of stuck.

Yield: 8 lip balm tubes

Salves and Balms

Making a homemade salve for the skin is much easier than most people think. They're a great way to fill your medicine cabinet and are much cheaper to make at home than purchasing, plus, you get to control the ingredients.

A balm is typically firmer than a salve—I use 3 parts oil to 1 part beeswax. A salve is typically softer and can have a ratio of 2 parts oil to 1 part beeswax, or even 2 parts oil with a cocoa or shea butter base and very little, if any, beeswax.

You will need a tin or glass container to store your salves and balms. I recommend going with a smaller Mason jar that allows you to get your fingers all the way to the bottom to scoop out the last of the salve and balm. Jelly jars work great.

When you're ready to make your salve, place the oil and beeswax in a double broiler or a large Pyrex measuring bowl over a smaller saucepan. Place a few inches of water in the lower pot and heat to a low boil.

Place a spoon or small saucer in the freezer.

Stir the oil and beeswax together until it's completely melted and in a liquid state. Test your salve by dropping a few drops onto the frozen spoon or saucer and placing it back in the freezer or fridge for a minute. Add more beeswax to make it firmer or more oil to make it softer.

Remove from heat and add in any essential oils (if using), stir, and pour into desired containers. Allow salve to cool and set. Store salve in a dark and cool space when not in immediate use for the longest shelf life.

Skin-Soothing Salve

> 1 ounce calendula-infused olive oil
> 1 ounce lavender-infused oil
> 1 ounce coconut oil or shea butter
> 1 ounce beeswax
> 10 to 15 drops lavender essential oil (optional)

Combine oils and beeswax in a double boiler over low heat and melt. When everything is liquefied, stir together and remove from heat. Allow to cool slightly and stir in essential oil. Pour into a tin or small jelly jar and allow to cool.

There are many herbs to choose from to infuse your oils with in the making of the salves. The addition of essential oils can also be used—just do your due diligence. Also, make sure and test a small area of skin when using a new herb in case you have allergies.

Popular Herb Choices:

- Arnica and peppermint for sore joints and muscles
- Chamomile, calendula, comfrey, and plantain for skin issues

You can use a single herb or combine them to your preference. It's up to you!

Peppermint Chocolate Body Lotion

We know our skin is our biggest organ and it absorbs what we put on it. Many of the lotions and creams you buy at the store have preservatives, fillers, and not so nice ingredients in them.

I don't know about you, but whenever I use store-bought lotion, it seems my skin never stays moisturized for long. I'm having to constantly reapply.

When you look at the ingredient list on most store-bought products, one of the first things listed is water. Water is a filler ingredient and it also causes the need for more preservatives in order to keep it from growing bacteria and to stay shelf stable. Plus, while water is essential for us to consume, it doesn't help moisturize our skin on the outside.

This homemade lotion can be made with just a few ingredients in very little time, and because we're not using fillers it's ultra-moisturizing to the skin. I like the addition of peppermint to this homemade lotion (it's really a cream) because peppermint is soothing to irritated skin and it smells divine with the cocoa butter. But you can customize this to any scents and herbs you wish. That's the true beauty of handmade.

2 ounces peppermint-infused olive oil
    (may sub in any other oil of your choice)
2 ounces shea butter
2 ounces cocoa butter
2 ounces coconut oil
10 to 15 drops peppermint essential oil (optional)

Heat up your double boiler.

Measure out your oils and butters and place them in the double boiler. Stir frequently until melted.

Remove from heat and pour into a food processor bowl or your stand mixer bowl. Move to the fridge to cool.

After 20 to 30 minutes, when oil is cooled but not solidified, add the drops of peppermint essential oil (don't worry about stirring it in; it will be fully whipped in the final stage. Place back in fridge until oil has softly set.

You want it to be soft enough that you can poke your finger in it, but not so soft there's still liquid beneath the surface.

When oil is set, place the bowl on the food processor and blend for about 4 minutes, until the oils turn creamy and soft. You may need to stop part way through and scrape down the sides. When finished, place into a glass container.

This is greasier than regular lotion when you first put it on, but it soaks in within a few minutes and leaves the skin super soft. If you're in the dead of summer or live where it's really hot, you may want to store this in the fridge if it starts to melt. I haven't had that issue.

Other popular scent combinations you may wish to try would be lavender or sweet orange. Sweet orange is not considered to be photo-toxic like many of the citrus oils. Always use citrus oils with care if applying to the skin as most can cause serious burns due to phototoxicity.

Herbal Bath Salts

One of the easiest ways to use your herbs is to make herbal bath salts. Many times when we think of using herbs we think of cooking, teas, and tinctures. However, your skin is your biggest organ, and it absorbs whatever it contacts.

Bath salts aren't anything new, but they're much cheaper to make at home, and you can choose what herbal and essential oil blend you'd like to make. Taking a warm bath in the evening is a great way to help relax before bedtime.

It's thought a warm bath will raise your body temperature, so when you get out and your body temperature falls (which happens naturally in the evening as your body prepares for rest) it may help your body become ready for sleep. The warm water also helps to relax stressed, tired, and sore muscles.

Adding bath salts puts aromatherapy into play with the addition of the herbs. Epsom salts are the main ingredient in bath salts. Except they're not really a salt. They're large crystals of magnesium sulfate. Our bodies need a proper level of magnesium to function properly. And some studies show magnesium may offer help with insomnia.[19]

Magnesium is one of the most important minerals in our bodies and helps regulate hundreds of enzymes in our bodies. It helps the proper function of our cardiovascular and endocrine systems as well as our brain and neurotransmission.[20] To sum it up, it's a pretty big deal in keeping us healthy on a whole lot of levels.

An Epsom salt bath can help increase your magnesium levels. Plus, any excuse to lounge in the tub for a half hour or so is a definite plus in my book.

You can use straight Epsom salts, especially if you're sensitive to scents, but it's fun to create different scent combinations and these make great gifts to give. You can choose to use essential oils, herbs, or a combination to create your bath salts.

Epsom salts can be found at almost any grocery store and pharmacy. You can purchase them in large bags or small containers. I keep a two-pound bag on hand.

Baking soda (sodium bicarbonate) is added to help soothe irritated skin, acts as a water conditioner, and helps leave skin feeling extra silky.

2 cups Epsom salts
½ cup baking soda
Sea salt (optional)
3 to 4 T. herb of choice (optional)
10 to 20 drops essential oil (optional)

Wash and rinse fresh herbs and let dry on an absorbent towel. Some favorite herbs for aiding relaxation are calendula, chamomile, and lavender. Rosemary and peppermint are good choices to help soothe tired and sore muscles. Chop finely with a sharp knife and stir into sea salt. Once combined, add to your Epsom salts. You can play around and do half sea salt and half Epsom salts, or adjust the ratio to your liking.

Mix all of this together and store in a clean Mason jar. Add 1 cup to bath water. To help dissolve the salts, pour them under the running water while the bath is drawing.

Never add essential oils directly to bath water, as they won't disperse. By adding them to the Epsom salts first, they're able to dissolve into the water. Otherwise you'll create an oil slick on top of the water. Always use essential oils with caution—less is more. Some oils, like peppermint, cinnamon, and other warm oils can burn the skin if applied directly without dilution (and some should never be applied to the skin or used in the bath). Do some research on the essential oil you select.

5 Old-Time Remedies That Work

I bet when you came down with the sniffles or common ailments as a child, your mother or grandmother had a bunch of different remedies she'd recommend. Some of them are plain odd and really have no place except for the fondness of telling the tale. But these old-time remedies do have a place in our home.

1. *Chicken soup is good for a cold.* Grandma knew her stuff on this one. Chicken soup is good for a cold and there's

science to prove it, even though we homesteaders knew it
before they did. The *New York Times* reports that chicken
soup can help reduce upper respiratory symptoms.[21]
Homemade chicken soup made with traditional bone
broth and lots of vegetables is going to be even more
beneficial. Whenever fall rolls around and we move into
cold and flu season, I recommend stocking up on your
stock.

2. *Baking soda for a bee sting.* My daughter was stung by a
   bee. The sting itself wasn't hurting (odd but very happy
   outcome), however she was itching it like crazy. I mixed
   up a paste of baking soda and water and applied it directly
   to the sting. It took away the itching and she was back to
   playing and running around in no time. *Note:* If you're
   allergic to bees or suspect an allergic reaction, get yourself
   to a doctor or emergency room immediately.

3. *Inhaling steam.* When your nose is congested and you
   feel like you can't breathe, take a hot shower or fill a sink
   or pot with hot water and make a tent. Take a towel and
   cover your head with it while leaning over the hot water,
   trapping the steam and allowing you to breathe it in, for
   a few minutes. Make sure you use commonsense and
   don't burn yourself. The steam will help loosen up your
   congestion and allow you to cough up the ick easier. Many
   people like to add a few drops of peppermint or eucalyptus
   oil to the water, but just the hot water itself will help. You
   could also add crushed peppermint leaves to the water,
   making an herbal steam. Menthol (derived from the mint
   family) is often used in humidifiers and as aromatherapy,
   and you can try adding a vaporizer or diffusing the oil to
   help. However, some small children and others may have
   sensitivities to peppermint and especially eucalyptus, so it's
   not recommended to use this method with infants or small

children. Watch for any signs of irritation when using this method of adding in the menthol family to your steam.

4. *Honey as a cough suppressant.* Who knew that sugar could actually be taken as medicine? But not just any old sugar. Only if you're using good raw honey can you call it medicine. A cup of warm honey tea with a bit of lemon doesn't just help warm you up, it actually relieves your cough. Honey is now being recommended as a cough suppressant in the medical community instead of over-the-counter products. (Again, we homesteaders were ahead of the curve on this one.) Is there anything cooler than being able to use your food storage as your medicine cabinet too? I prefer local raw honey for all of the benefits it offers. If you can find a local beekeeper or local source, I'd go with that, otherwise look for raw honey at your local co-op or grocery store. Many people like to infuse their honey with herbs or spices for flavor and further medicinal properties. To retain all of the benefits of honey, raw or unpasteurized honey is best. *Note:* Do not give honey to children under a year old due to the risk of botulism.

5. *Ginger for nausea and upset stomach.* If you had an upset stomach, there's a good chance your granny might have given you some ginger tea. For years people have used ginger to treat digestive and stomach ailments, and some studies have shown it to be beneficial while others aren't as conclusive. *Note:* Ginger may help soothe an upset stomach, but if you're on blood thinning medications or have a blood clotting disorder, you should consult with a medical professional before using.

Simplify

Has anyone else noticed a very odd cycle in mainstream modern society? We bemoan having to work so much, yet we constantly buy things that fill up our homes, so we purge and declutter, taking boxes to donate, and yet the cycle never seems to stop.

We almost seem addicted to stuff. And I'm not pointing fingers. My home has a fair number of things in it, including a bag of things to donate to the thrift shop, at this very moment.

Not only are we tied to a whole lot of things, but our schedules are packed to the brim. We run around like a hen with a coyote in the chicken coop most of the time. No wonder so many of us are tired, exhausted, stretched tight, and ready to snap. And even if we think disorder and chaos don't bother us, they do.

I've always said, "A little bit of clutter doesn't bother me. I can't stand dirty, but I don't mind stuff." Some of you cringed when you read that, while others of you just hollered, "Amen, sister!"

That's how my home has rolled—reorganizing areas of disorder and clutter, dusting and wiping up the crumbs with a daily sweep of the main floor. When things are really hectic, sometimes that includes shoving a pile to the side to find enough room to work and getting done the must-haves.

My home would never have been on an episode of *Hoarders*, but it certainly wouldn't have been gracing any magazine features that showcase neat and tidy living. In the back of my mind as I sat down to work was the knowledge that I needed to tackle my computer desk, the laundry room, and other areas niggled like a stray hair down my back.

Nothing will dissuade you from doing something faster than knowing that you have to first clean off an area before you even begin.

With all of our modern conveniences it's been estimated we have the equivalent of several servants. We can wash our clothes with the flip of a switch, clean our dishes with the push of a button, and throw our supper into a slow cooker and have dinner ready when we walk through the door. In other words, we have it pretty good compared to life hundreds of years ago.

Yet many of us struggle with too much stuff, the feeling of never having enough time, and the sensation of drowning in our to-do lists. We run from one thing to the next, with always the threat of needing to do more looming over our heads like a buzzing fly.

We've forgotten the art of enjoying the moment and being satisfied with less.

There are many articles and books out there on decluttering, but what I've found is we need to truly decide what it is we prioritize in life and match our actions to it.

> Seek first his kingdom and his righteousness, and all these things will be given to you as well. Therefore do not worry about tomorrow, for tomorrow will worry about itself. Each day has enough trouble of its own (Matthew 6:33-34).

How to Simplify Your Life

We really don't require that much to survive. When we get down to the basics we need shelter, water, and food.

How is it most of us have this in abundance, yet still feel like we're barely making it?

Our homes should be a haven, a sanctuary, a place we love to be and gladly open our doors and hearts for others to come in and feel loved. A simplified life starts with a simplified heart.

We have to know what it is we really want. For me, that is serving God and seeking Him daily, honoring Him with my actions and choices. Next is loving my family and creating a home that they, and I, want to be in. Next is being faithful to my calling and gifts God has given me with my blog, podcast, and writing.

All of my other goals, or life themes, stem from these three mission statements.

Once we know what is important to us, it becomes easier to weed out the things that aren't that important or don't line up with our goals.

I look back to the folks who went through the Great Depression and the pioneers of old. They had hardships, they went through tough times, they went without a lot of things we have today, but many of them had a form of contentment and joy society as a whole seems to be lacking.

When we go through hardships we learn it's the simple things that matter. Not the latest trendy wall color or must-have accessory for the season.

I realized the condition of my home was keeping me from truly enjoying it. Please don't mistake this for a call to legalism where if your house isn't perfectly kept and tidy you're failing. That is not what I'm getting at here.

If you walk into your home and clutter, piles of papers, or other items make your shoulders droop, then it's time do something about it. If you never have time to get your home in order then you need to declutter your schedule.

Simplifying the Kitchen

Let's start with the kitchen. The majority of my time at home is spent in this room. I have found the only way to truly declutter a room or area is to take everything out or off the surface so I'm starting with a clean slate. Otherwise, I end up constantly reorganizing the same chaos.

When I'm evaluating whether or not to keep an item, I use these questions to help me decide if I really need to keep it.

1. Do I use it regularly?
2. Do I have another item that could be used in its place?
3. If needed, could I borrow this item once a year from someone else?

For example, I had a punch bowl but hardly ever used it. I also had a glass pitcher and glass gallon container with a spigot for making sun tea. I can easily make punch in the glass pitcher or sun tea container. I donated the punch bowl.

1. **Countertops.** Only leave items on the countertops that you use frequently (preferably daily or several times a week) or are too heavy to lift in and out of a cupboard. If it can go in a cupboard easily instead of on the counter, put it in the cupboard. I keep my grain mill and blender in a cupboard instead of on the counter, but my KitchenAid mixer gets to stay on the counter.

2. **Cupboards.** Take out everything and wipe down the cupboard. Evaluate every item for either the keep or donate pile. Will you ever have need of more than two pie plates at one time?

3. **Create stations.** Now that you've gone through everything, don't put it back in the same way. My cupboards act as stations for different items. Example: I have a baking cupboard station that houses baking ingredients and a baking cupboard station that houses my pie plates, wire racks, cake pans, and mixing bowls. Look at your countertop again, now that you've purged some cupboard space. Is there anything still on the counter that could go in a cupboard with its station?

4. **Organize the items in the cupboard.** Put items less used in the back of the cupboard. More frequent items go in front. Try to take advantage of vertical space. Stack larger pans on the bottom and nest smaller ones on top. For my

baking and cookie sheets I got a wire pantry organizer rack. It holds all of my baking sheets, including my stoneware, on their sides.

5. **Organize the flow.** If you've ever cooked in a restaurant, you know how important it is to have the items you go through the fastest up close and center. When you have customers waiting on their dinner and more orders coming in, you can't spend time running from one end of the kitchen to the other for supplies or tools (your feet will ache enough at the end of the shift). Create the same type of flow in your own home kitchen. Example: I used to have my wooden mixing spoons, whisk, ladle, spatula, and rolling pin on the opposite side of the kitchen from the stove. Whenever I was cooking I had to walk from the stove and around the island to get to the drawer where these were kept. After clearing off my countertop so I had space, I was able to use an open utensil crock to house all these items. It has saved me an incredible amount of time not having to walk around for these or dig through the drawer to find them. Plus, functional decorations are a must in the kitchen. Look at where you're storing items and decide if that's really the best place for them. I previously kept my flour and sugar in canisters in the cupboard. But when you're cooking from scratch, you end up getting them out multiple times a day—especially the sugar during jam and jelly making season. I invested in the large Ball storage canisters so they can sit on the counter next to the cookie jar where our knives used to sit. The knives got moved to the other side of the kitchen closer to the sink, where the majority of chopping and slicing happen.

6. **Create a shoppable pantry.** How many times have you bought something at the store because you thought you were out of it, only to find the same item later buried at

the back of the pantry? (Hoping I'm not the only one here.) When you go to the grocery store, you know all the spices are in one section, cooking oils, baking supplies, etc. You immediately know when they're sold out of an item because there's a glaring hole on the shelf. Treat your pantry and cupboards the same way. Designate one area for like goods. Arrange spices and herbs alphabetically. Again, go vertical to maximize space and efficiency when possible. Most spice and herb containers are fairly short, so you can double the amount of visual space (making it easy to see all your spices and herbs) by using shelf risers. With the use of shelf risers, I created an additional two shelves in my spice and seasoning cupboard. I prefer to use glass storage containers whenever possible, so I can see at a glance when I'm almost out of something and what's in it. Generally, I purchase our rice, quinoa, sugar, salt, spices and herbs I don't grow myself, pasta, and wheat berries in bulk. I use glass canisters and half gallon Mason jars to house these. We grow our own dried beans and these go in quart-sized Mason jars. When I open up this cupboard, I can easily see which container I want, when one is low, and plus, everything just looks better in a Mason jar.

Great Depression-Era Tip

Instead of purchasing ingredients to make what you want, look at what you already have in the cupboard and come up with a meal. You might just find you've invented your family's newest favorite.

7. **Cookbooks.** Am I the only one who is a collector of recipes and cookbooks? I have an affinity for antique

cookbooks. They hold many tidbits and recipes that are truly made from scratch without processed ingredients. I also have several modern cookbooks, especially my canning ones, to make sure I'm up-to-date on safety. If you're like me, you'll soon realize your cookbook shelf is spilling over. You'll also realize you use some often, some for maybe one or two recipes, and some never. For cookbooks you only use a few recipes from every now and then, copy down the recipe and put that cookbook in the donate pile. Cookbooks I use every week are arranged in a wire basket on the open shelf of my island to act as functional decoration. My favorite vintage cookbooks I use some of the time, I have arranged on the shelf above my writing desk (in the corner of the kitchen), and the rest were donated or given to people I thought would have a better use for them. If you're unsure if you can really part with an item, put it in a box or bag in the garage or a corner of your closet and see if you ever go and get that item. If several weeks or months go by and you haven't retrieved it, you can safely say good-bye.

8. **Decorations and knickknacks.** This can be a hard one. Most of us want our homes to reflect our likes and dislikes. We don't want a sterile environment with no personality or a replica of a store showroom. But over the years, our tastes may change (I like to think they are being refined), and we tend to hold onto things without thinking about it. We have open space on top of our cupboards, a perfect display area. When I was a little girl I created a hope chest. Our current and only set of blue willow dishes were carefully collected piece by piece. I also collected replica vintage tins. My kitchen felt overflowing. Too busy. After purging everywhere else, the upper shelves and decorations were next. I realized I was only displaying the tins because I'd had them forever. They really weren't something I loved

and I certainly wouldn't pick them up again at a thrift store. I kept the blue willow dishes but donated the tins. When going through your décor here are my best tips: Take everything down and off shelves and the wall. Wash it (we won't say how thick the dust is) and evaluate each piece. One of the best tips I've ever gotten on whether or not to keep a piece was by Kathi Lipp, author of *Clutter Free,* and it was to ask yourself this question, Would you buy it again? Would you go to the store right now and pay money for that same piece to replace it if it were damaged or broken?" This has been invaluable advice in helping me decide what to get rid of and what to keep. Some pieces I'll keep because they have sentimental value. I have only two things from my grandmother, and one is a vintage piece of blue glassware—it goes front and center. You do have to be careful of keeping too many sentimental pieces, though. Only keep it if you truly love it and it brings you joy when you look at it. Keeping something just because it belonged to Great-Aunt Edna even though you don't really like it isn't worth it to me.

9. **Use functional décor.** A lot of times your display or decoration pieces can also serve a purpose. In the kitchen I have an open shelving unit that houses a covered enamelware roasting pan with a pretty patterned tea towel next to it and my flour sifter. It's put together to make a display, but I can—and do—use each piece when needed. My earthenware crock houses potatoes but also looks charming on the shelf while doing so. A vintage towel hangs from the oven door to use as an oven mitt, cover a fresh loaf of bread straight out of the oven, or dry hands on. But if you have a favorite piece that serves no function other than bringing you joy by looking at it, then that is a purpose well served too.

10. **Cleaning cupboard.** How is it that the area we store the things to make the rest of our house clean can become such an area of disarray? Our first rule is the same as for all of the other spaces: Take everything out. Look at the cleaning products. Have you honestly used them in the last few months? If the answer is no, pitch them. I don't like using harsh chemicals in my home. I use baking soda and vinegar to clean almost all surfaces in our home.

The best way to keep everything tidy and neat is to make sure everything has a home. I have a small caddy that houses the dusting and cleaning rags. Another one holds the spray bottles with our all-purpose cleaner and furniture polish along with the extra bottle of dish soap and dishwasher soap. I keep it in the cupboard under the kitchen sink. It's so much easier if you can see everything when you open the cupboard.

The Living Room

Besides the kitchen, the living room is usually one of the most-used rooms in the home. We always spend the evening together in our living room after supper. If company comes over, usually we'll congregate in the living room.

1. **Media/Entertainment Center.** We don't actually own an entertainment center, but we do have CDs, DVDs, games, and similar paraphernalia. Our television hangs on the wall, and I have an antique wooden shipping trunk beneath it that holds photo albums, manuals, and lesser-used media. Regardless of where your items are stored, follow these steps: Start by pulling out all your movies, CDs, and games. Donate any you know you won't watch or have had for more than a year and haven't gotten around to watching or playing with. If you haven't

watched/listened to/played them in that amount of time, you're most likely not going to. Have your kids go through their games; chances are they've outgrown some of them or no longer play them anymore. Keep only your favorites. For easy cleanup and storage, designate one area (we like to use baskets) for each media type. All of my kids' games go in one basket along with controllers and game pieces.

2. **Magazines/books.** These are easy to let pile up, especially periodicals. If you see a particular article or recipe in a magazine you want to try, clip out that section and keep it in a binder. Books are cherished things and can be hard to part with. If I'll read the book again (a sign of a truly good book), then I'll keep it. But if I've had the book for a while and still haven't gone back to reference it or reread it for enjoyment, it goes into the donation pile. Choose a designated area for your books and once it's full, it's full. This will help you be ruthless in culling titles you don't really love. It also makes you keep them to a manageable level for the space you have.

3. **Coffee and end tables.** Clear off everything and dust or wash the surface. My guess is a lot of things get piled on your end tables, especially the one right next to where you sit (not just my house, right?). If it's always the same items, (mine happens to be my Kindle and Bible), think about getting a basket to set them in that slides right under the table or can sit next to the chair. It makes it easier to clean and the room looks tidier when you don't have things on every surface. Decide if the items serve a function, need a designated home (and create one), or can be gotten rid of.

4. **Furniture.** We have a wood burning fireplace. For convenience we had a small wood box next to the stove and another box for the kindling. While practical, it added to the number of items in the living room as well

as my having to constantly sweep up the bark and other debris that came with wood. We set the two firewood boxes outside on our back deck. The firewood was only a few more steps to reach and I no longer had a set of boxes to clean up around and clutter up the fireplace. Along the wall that held our television, I kept a trunk with two end tables. One of the end tables held a photo and a few other knickknacks. It wasn't really serving a purpose. I hung the photo on the wall and decided I didn't love the knickknacks (remember our rule from the kitchen— would you buy it again right now?). I gave the table to friends who'd just moved into a bigger home and needed one. Really evaluate whether you're using all the pieces in your room or using them to their best advantage. You might find you've held on to a piece simply because you've always had it. I've found that by having less in our living room, it's easier to keep clean, and I really see the pieces I love. When I enter the room, my gaze is able to focus on the things I cherish rather than on all the stuff because I narrowed down the number of things to those that matter most to me. When we turn our focus on the things we love, we create a home of joy and simplicity.

5. **Blankets/throw pillows.** I like nothing more than snuggling up under a cozy blanket with a good book in our living room. Throw pillows and blankets are a must in our home. Not only are they functional, but they can offer decoration all on their own. I especially love quilts. They are a testament to a bygone era, where people used what they had to create something functional and beautiful. When people worked for their very survival and the means or the supplies to engage in the arts was hard to come by, they used scraps of clothing and leftover material to create true masterpieces. Beautiful quilts are still being produced today, and I consider quilting an art form.

I first learned to quilt from my mother and grandmother. When I was eight years old, my grandmother had hooks in the ceiling of her log cabin up the road from us. I wore a trail in the grass and under the barbwire fence from our house to hers. My mother would stand at one fence and watch until I slid under the fence where my grandmother waited for me. A large quilting frame hung suspended from the ceiling, a quilt pulled tight between the wooden frames. Two chairs flanked the sides of the blanket where she taught a friend how to quilt. A desire blossomed in my heart to follow in the path of my grandmother and mother, the flash of a silver needle pulling thread between layers of fabric to create an embrace of warmth on chilly eves. A friend of the family took me to pick out fabric to start my first quilt. My mother enlarged the pattern for the traditional Flower Garden quilt so my small fingers and smaller patience would be able to finish it sooner than a standard pattern. She sewed the first flower by hand with me, showing me how to make small and even stitches to bind the pieces together.

Handmade quilts are threads that tether us to the people who made them and to the past. I've come across quilts at thrift stores and flea markets, and I always wonder about the story of the person who stitched it. One of my favorite ways to display quilts is on a ladder. The rungs make excellent rods to drape the folded quilts or blankets over. You can prop the ladder up against the wall or use a painter's ladder that will stand independently. The blankets look neat and tidy but are easy to remove to cover up a sick child, snuggle with a good book or loved one, or keep warm. When I'm displaying my blankets and quilts, I can more easily see which blankets aren't pleasing to the eye and cull them for other projects, narrowing down what I have on display in our home.

Simplifying the Bathroom

1. **Countertops.** You know the drill—take everything off.
   Wipe them clean. Look at everything you had on your
   countertops. I have a basket at my sink to hold my face
   wash, face cream, and lotions. If you're like me, you likely
   have a few—or a whole lot—of those items you haven't
   used in weeks. But we hate to throw out something we
   spent money on, don't we? If you haven't used that cream
   on a daily or every-other-day basis, throw it away. You're
   not using it because it either didn't work as well as you'd
   hoped, or you just plain aren't using it. Don't keep things
   you're not using. Put back only the items on your counter
   you're using on an everyday basis and that don't fit well in
   a drawer or cupboard. Ladies, go through your makeup.
   Mascara is a breeding ground for bacteria and should be
   replaced every 3 to 6 months. If you have mascara older
   than that (and has been opened and used), throw it away.
   You likely have tubes of lipstick, eyeshadow, blush, and
   foundation that you don't use because they're not the
   right shade. Throw them away. If they haven't been the
   right shade in the last 6 months, you're not going to wake
   up one morning and decide they're fantastic. Keep only
   the makeup, skin care, and body care products you use
   frequently.

2. **Drawers and cupboards.** Take it all out, clean out the
   drawers, and don't put everything back until you've
   assessed it all with the criteria we've discussed. Create
   a spot and home for everything you're going to keep,
   preferably in a container. A small, wide mouth canning
   jar is wonderful for your hair ties, bobby pins, and small
   things. A small wastebasket or box can hold your hair dyer,
   curling iron, straightener, and the like. Try to use things
   you already have on hand. This is a good time to look at
   your first aid kit and make a list of any items that need to

be replaced or you're almost out of. Plus, toss anything that's way past its expiration date.

3. **Linen Closet.** Go through your washcloths and towels. Any that have holes in them or are almost threadbare should go into the rag bin. Look at your sheets, blankets, pillows, and pillowcases. If there are any that no longer fit the beds you have or are mismatched (we always tend to wear out the bottom sheet first), either put them in your scrap bag or rag bin, or donate if you don't think you'll ever use the fabric for anything. But sheets are a great source of a large amount of fabric in one solid piece and can be used to back quilts.

4. **Tub and shower.** I'll bet you have a few containers of shampoo and conditioner that are almost empty or you haven't used in a while. Either consolidate them into a bottle and use it up or toss them. Check your razors, and if they're dull, throw them out or change the blade. Put bath bombs, bath salts, bubble bath, and other bathing items in a caddy or basket. Having them corralled together helps make cleaning easier. But keep only the items you're using. Consider installing a shelf to house items above the toilet. This is a great place for extra towels and toiletries.

Simplifying the Laundry Room

1. **Purge.** Somehow my laundry room becomes the dumping ground for things I don't know what to do with at the moment. Remove everything from the shelves, top of the dryer, and any other nook or cranny. Decide what really belongs there.

2. **Create a designated area.** If everything has a home and specified spot, it's easier to clean up and keep things neat.

If something isn't in its spot, you know where it should go and when it's not there.

3. **Go vertical.** Instead of having my stain remover and clothespins sitting on top of the dryer, I installed a wire basket on the wall right above the dryer. The basket can easily be taken down and used if needed, but it also houses my laundry softener, wool drier balls, and basket of rags. Instead of a shelf, try hanging a crate with its bottom to the wall, as you'll get two areas to place things on because both the top and the bottom sides of the crate become shelves.

4. **Go through your supplies.** Chances are you have old bottles of things that are almost gone or you no longer use. Even though I no longer use certain products after having gone to a more natural home, I still found some old bottles way at the back of the laundry shelf. I knew I wouldn't use them so I threw them away.

Simplify the Bedroom

The bedroom should be a place that evokes rest and peace. I don't know about you, but a ton of clutter and mess does not make me feel restful.

The biggest area of clutter in my bedroom happens from the overflow of my closet and dresser. Anyone else have the clothes issue?

During the Great Depression, most people only had a few outfits to pick from. You would have your dress clothes, usually only one or two outfits, which were reserved for church and special occasions. You would have one to three everyday outfits, and one or two work or chore outfits.

Many people only had one or two pairs of shoes and oftentimes didn't wear them at home to keep from wearing out the soles. When holes were worn through the soles and they couldn't afford a replacement pair, they'd put cardboard in the bottom of the shoe.

While I'm grateful that most of us are able to afford more than three total outfits and can replace our shoes when they wear out, we can all adopt some of the following tips:

1. **Scale back on your clothes.** Keep track of which outfits you're actually wearing on a weekly basis. If you only have clothes that fit you right now and you feel good in, going into your closet without having to waste time wading through the items you don't wear will save you time and space. Many people are familiar with this hanger trick: Place all your hangers facing one direction and when you wear that item, switch the direction of the hanger. After two months (or a time limit that you decide), if the hanger hasn't been switched, hence the clothing item not getting actual wear time, it goes into the donation pile. Other people have a strict number of clothes they can have in their closet at one time. This helps with impulse buys and bringing anything new in, because if something new comes in, something else has to go. One caveat: If you live in an area with definite seasons, you'll have some items that are only worn in winter and others that are worn only in summer. These can go in their own seasonal capsule, and winter clothes won't count toward the summer ones and vice versa.

   Also keep track of the number of shoes you have. You know those pairs that look amazing but after ten minutes you're kicking them off because they pinch your toes so bad? Get rid of them!

2. **A place for everything.** I feel like this could be a motto on a cup because we've been saying it so much through the book, but it's so true. If everything has a designated home, it's easy to see when something is out of place. I prefer to group my clothes together. All of the jeans in one spot, sweatshirts, dresses, etc. When they're all together it's easier to get dressed, and it's quickly apparent when you have

too many of an item. Do we really need 15 pairs of jeans? Get a scarf hanger (or you can put shower curtain rings on a regular hanger and thread the scarfs through the rings) if you have more than one or two scarves. Hang up your jewelry or find a way to organize it so you can quickly see what you have to wear at a glance.

3. **Children's rooms.** Toys. Yes, that elephant in the room. Depending upon the child's age, I have them go through their things with me. Usually we've battled too often on them cleaning up their rooms, and they're as tired of the struggle as I am. We go through every item, and I ask them if they really play with it (but Mom has final say). Some things have gotten broken and can't be fixed or aren't worth being fixed, others they've outgrown, and some they've never really played with. Everything comes out of the toy closet or off the shelves, same as the other rooms. We find baskets or boxes (they can be cardboard boxes you label) to house smaller toys, especially things with many small pieces. If an item is still in good shape, I will first try to sell it online in a local Facebook group designated for selling and/or bartering, or in a garage sale. This really helps motivate the kids, and I know if they'd rather have money than the item, they really aren't using it or don't care about it. It also shows them that just because you try to sell something doesn't mean someone else will buy it. Deal is, if it goes up for sale, even if it doesn't sell, we're still getting rid of it. I truly believe when kids have too many toys, they are overwhelmed and rarely play with most of them. It may be they can't find a toy if the room is a mess, but if they have fewer choices and the choices are things they really like, they'll play with them more. And if their possessions have a clear place to go, children will be able to tidy up on their own more easily.

We've just talked a lot about throwing things away that you're not using. We need to clean everything out in order to focus and find the items that matter. But sometimes when we go through belongings, it helps us to look at them in a new light.

Some of the things you decide to throw away may serve a better purpose in another room or in another way. This isn't an excuse to hold on to possessions but rather an opportunity to see if they can serve a better purpose elsewhere.

During the Great Depression, people couldn't afford to purchase items new. They learned to be creative and reuse things they already owned.

Great Depression-Era Tip

The Great Depression still reaches its fingers through time, both as a warning and as a lesson. My grandparents lived through the Great Depression, and though my father was a young boy, he still remembers those early years. It was an event with lifelong lessons that those who lived through will always carry with them.

They knew what it was to go without, to truly go without. Their creativity and DIY mentality and lifestyle were a must. They learned how to take very little and turn it into more. Items were used in multiple ways or repurposed.

If you had to purchase something, you first looked at home for something you could repurpose, trade or barter, or purchase used.

Find Ways to Repurpose Things

One reader said her grandmother taught her to wash out plastic bags. During the Depression they didn't use plastic bags, but in today's time we can learn to wash and reuse things instead of use one time and toss. Wash bags out and then turn them inside out to dry. I use parchment paper when baking instead of aluminum foil. I reuse the parchment paper every time I bake bread a minimum of 2 to 3 times before throwing it away. Most things can be reused more than we currently do.

Take old socks and make them into dust rags or dusting mitts. Same thing with old towels and washcloths—these make excellent cleaning rags and can be used time and time again.

Learn how to mend clothes. Many clothes will come apart at the seams or have a small tear, but with a needle and thread, they are as good as new again. Knowing how to hem a pair of pants or a dress means you can use a hand-me-down from an older sibling and turn it into something wearable for younger children.

I've done this with some of my sundresses for my daughter. Simply shorten the straps, take it in under the arms on each side, and hem if necessary.

If you have some shirts beyond repair, snip off the buttons and save them. It used to be that every home had a button box (anyone else remember this from Laura Ingalls?). Those buttons can be expensive and can be used later for craft and sewing projects.

Small children often outgrow their clothes before they wear them out. Look through the fabrics and keep any pretty prints, especially cotton, that can be turned into a quilt or patched together for a pillow cover. Just like button boxes, generations past kept a fabric bag or basket. You can cut out the worn or stained parts and keep the remaining fabric for quilting, crafts, and patching items.

Use handkerchiefs for colds and wiping noses. That scrap fabric works well for these projects and you're not paying money on items you use once and throw away.

There are many videos online that will show you how to turn a

T-shirt into an easy and simple tote bag by sewing the bottom closed and cutting off the sleeves and collar to create two straps.

Old sweaters can be turned into cozy pillow covers, and the sleeves can be cut into boot socks or leg warmers or made into fingerless gloves by cutting a thumbhole. How about a hat? I simply took a hat I had, laid it on top of the sweater bottom, and cut around it, leaving enough of the sweater for seam allowance.

Back in the pioneer days, each day of the week was set to a certain task.

- Monday was wash day
- Tuesday was ironing day
- Wednesday was mending day
- Thursday market day
- Friday cleaning day
- Saturday baking day
- Sunday church and rest day

Most of us don't need an entire day to do all the laundry—hallelujah—and I don't know about you, but I rarely iron. Certainly not even once a month.

But scheduling things for a certain day and creating a routine will help us get done what we need to do and leave a balance of rest, provided we devote a day and time to it. I tend to do laundry throughout the week so it never builds up. Plus, because I work outside the home, I can't necessarily devote whole days to doing an entire cleaning.

However, we can devote certain chores to certain days to create a schedule. For example, filing papers could be done every Thursday in place of churning. Baking and meal prep could certainly be relegated to one major day for the entire week.

There are some chores that need to be done every day, but for others, having a designated day in homage to home management from years ago is certainly a great plan.

* * *

When I was a little girl, we rarely went out to eat. We didn't have much money—and even if we had, the nearest fast-food restaurants were close to an hour away.

Instead, my mom would let me and my friends play fast food. My dad had an old 1930 Ford Model A car (still does) with a rumble seat in the back. We would open the seat and climb up the fender into it. Mom would bring us out our food in folded brown paper bags and serve us our food like we were at a drive-through window.

Inside those crinkled, reused brown bags, our food was packed just like a real drive-through. Our hamburger or chicken was wrapped up in a paper towel, our fries in another towel, and our napkins at the bottom of the bag.

This was such a simple thing—one my mother could have easily brushed aside, saying she was too busy, but it clearly stands out in my memories. It taught me to look for contentment in unexpected places. Instead of focusing on being disappointed we couldn't actually go out to a real restaurant, she showed me how to be happy with what we did have. One of the best secrets to happiness in life is simply changing the delivery.

For example, I'm not particularly fond of getting up early. In fact, when I was younger, the rising sun and I did not meet unless absolutely forced. I had my routine worked out perfectly so that I only needed 15 minutes to get out the door upon waking on school mornings. When I didn't absolutely have to wake up, I could easily sleep until ten if not disturbed.

Those days are long gone, and I'm still not a natural morning person. I use my snooze button on the alarm regularly. (Did you know that if you hit it enough, eventually it gives up?)

Even though I'm not really a morning person, most mornings I rise between 5:45 and 6:15 to start my day. A far cry from the ten o'clock mornings of my youth. Instead of dreading my early morning risings, I remind myself of what they allow me to accomplish. I get to work on my writing. Many people never get to live out their dream, and

I'm lucky enough to be living mine. The wee-hour rendezvous with my computer acts like a shot of caffeine and propels me from my cozy bed. (Though I confess I'm still a tiny bit bleary-eyed for the first few sentences.)

If I focus on how tired I am, I'm much more likely to hit that snooze button. Again and again. It's all in the delivery of the way we view things that makes the difference. If we look for the bad, we will find it. If we look for the good, we will find it. They're both there, but the one we choose to focus on will be the one we experience.

> Finally, brothers and sisters, whatever is true, whatever is noble, whatever is right, whatever is pure, whatever is lovely, whatever is admirable—if anything is excellent or praiseworthy—think about such things (Philippians 4:8).

What we think about, the way we think about it, determines our happiness.

Chapter 6

Homespun Holidays

One of my favorite things to do at Christmastime is to decorate. I love the colors swirling about and the memories attached to certain treasured ornaments or decorations. When I was a little girl, my mother had a Christmas music box shaped like the front of the house with a little blond-haired girl in a red coat standing at the door with a small tree on the side that housed a tea light candle.

I pretended I was the little girl and adored winding up the music box (very carefully) to listen to it play. My mother gifted the music box to me when my daughter was small, and someday I'll pass it on to her.

Believe it or not, this homestead girl actually has a fake tree. We have a woodstove in our living room and a live tree only lasts a few weeks before it becomes a fire hazard, no matter how much water we keep in it.

We put our tree up two days after Thanksgiving, hence the need for a fake one. The kids and I spend the afternoon hanging up the ornaments and setting out our favorite decorations. Why is it that when you put the lights away, every single strand works, but after you bring them all out, there's always that one that doesn't?

But the real finale is when we turn on the lights. My husband strings up the lights on the outside of the house, and we always position the Christmas tree in the front window so you can see the lights from it shining out as well. We wait until it gets dark and then we all go outside for the lighting. Thankfully, we've not had a Griswald moment, and we've never blinded our neighbors or had complete light failure.

One afternoon I glanced at our Christmas tree. The lights weren't on yet as I tend to not plug them in until later in the day. All the ornaments were in place, the star crowning the top and the red skirt draped around the bottom. It was pretty, it had all of the components there, but it didn't have the same impact.

I plugged in the lights. Ornaments gleamed, the icy snowflakes glittered, and the lights twinkled. It was as if the Christmas spirit itself had entered the room.

Then it hit me. That is our life and world without Jesus.

We can have all the right things in place. We can look the part, go to church, quote the Bible, say the things society says are good and right, but without the true light of Jesus, we're just a dull imitation.

Or on the flip side, we can be a complete mess, with our latest mistake sitting front and center on our chest like a scarlet letter. Like a Christmas tree with gaping holes, chipped ornaments, and an angel with a broken wing. But when those lights come on, we no longer see all of that.

Instead, the light of Jesus is multiplied in the ornaments, and despite the chips, we no longer see the bare spots. The glow of His love not only covers up our sins, it washes them away, and He takes those broken spots and makes them into one big, beautiful light that reaches out to light the lives of others.

It's when Jesus comes into our midst, makes a home in our hearts, and lights us from within that we see the true splendor we were meant to be. Have you ever noticed that those who really love God just seem to have this inner glow, no matter what their age or circumstances?

> When Jesus spoke again to the people, he said, "I am the light of the world. Whoever follows me will never walk in darkness, but will have the light of life" (John 8:12).

How many of us have been like that unlit tree? God has already carefully chosen each decoration and facet about us. He's lovingly placed them just so in our lives, and He's waiting for us to turn on the light so we can see how beautiful we are and all of the gifts He's given us.

I don't know about you, but sometimes I have a hard time seeing all of the beauty He sees in me. I tend to focus on all the things I haven't gotten right, the times I've messed up, the shame of past sins instead of the grace and mercy of today.

Have you ever noticed that when one strand of lights on your tree burns out it's all you can see? It doesn't matter that the rest of the strands are twinkling, your eye can't help but notice that one broken strand. Immediately you go to work trying to find the burned-out bulb to fix it. Or perhaps you're not a wasting-any-time type of girl and pull out a brand new strand—no judgment here.

When we don't accept God's grace and mercy, we're walking around with burned-out lights on our tree.

God is longing to fix the strand. Immediately, He sees when one of His children is hurting or living in the shame of the past, but we have to trust Him enough to truly turn the light back on.

You are beautiful. Your past, your mistakes, your sins, all are washed white as snow once you accept Jesus as your Savior. He called you, knowing full well all of the things you've done and all of the things you will do, the good and the bad.

> He chose us in him before the creation of the world to be
> holy and blameless in his sight (Ephesians 1:4).

You are forgiven. You are called. You are His own and beloved. Turn the light on, my dear friend. Turn the light on.

Birthdays

It's funny how we view birthdays depending on our age. When we're little, we can't wait for our birthday and often proudly insert the half. I think my kids say they're "and a half" the day after their birthday.

Once we hit those middle years, sometimes we'd rather forget we've reached that milestone yet again.

Then as we gain some more wisdom with the years, we hopefully start to see that each birthday is a gift. God has given us another year to live out His plan for us. While it might not come in a box, wrapped in paper and tied with a bow, it is a gift, nonetheless. We get to decide what we'll do with said gift during the next 365 days—to let it sit on a shelf until the next year rolls around or make sure we get full life out of it.

When I was little, my birthday meant I got to pick what was for dinner. Choosing a favorite restaurant wasn't an option. This was our favorite *homemade* meal and dessert. We've carried the tradition on with our children, and it's fun to see which foods get swapped out as they grow older and which ones stay.

Chocolate Gravy

When you were growing up, did you have any favorite foods that weren't served very often? Whenever it showed up on the table, you knew it was something special.

My dad always talks about my grandmother serving biscuits with chocolate gravy on special days. His eyes light up at the memory. Unfortunately, I never got the recipe from my grandmother before she passed away, and I don't ever remember her serving it. My mom never made it either.

One year I was determined to surprise Dad with chocolate gravy for breakfast. Everyone should start their special day with a tasty surprise, right? I scoured my cookbooks and between a chocolate sauce recipe in my great-grandmother's *Watkins Cook Book* and a close friend, Sue Watts, who is an expert cook (everyone needs at least one or two friends in their life who are expert cooks), I tweaked the recipe a bit to make enough to smother biscuits.

I'm not sure who was more excited over the breakfast treat, Dad or me.

¼ cup melted butter
1 T. flour

½ cup sugar
¼ stp. salt
½ cup cocoa powder
¾ cup boiling water
1 cup milk
½ tsp. vanilla

Blend melted butter with flour in a saucepan over medium heat. Add sugar, salt, and cocoa powder. Whisk in boiling water and milk. Let milk get hot and remove pot from stove. Stir in vanilla. If you let it boil, it may thicken up like pudding.

Serve warm over biscuits. If you have any left over, it makes a great chocolate sauce for homemade chocolate milk or to serve over ice cream. Store in a small Mason jar in the fridge.

Birthday Cake

Another tradition surrounding birthdays since the day my kids were born is a homemade birthday cake. Some years they've tested mom's decorating skills from a John Deere tractor cake to Mickey (and then Minnie) Mouse and even a Darth Vader cake.

We never purchase boxed cake mixes—but if you've made it this far in the book, I have a feeling you knew that was coming. Truthfully, you can make an awesome cake at home without worrying if you've got a mix in the cupboard or needing to run to the store.

Cake Making Tips:

1. Room-temperature butter, eggs, and milk will give you a lighter-textured cake.

2. Sift the flour. Seriously, I know this seems so old-school and who has time for it, but it really only takes a few minutes and you can tell the difference.

3. Try using cake flour—but there's no need to buy it. Instead,

for every cup of flour, place 2 tablespoons of cornstarch (I use only organic corn products) in the bottom of your measuring cup and then fill normally with all-purpose flour.

4. Grease and flour your pans beforehand.

5. Preheat your oven and make sure the rack is smack dab in the middle.

This recipe is adapted from *Betty Crocker's Picture Cookbook*.

⅔ cup soft/room temperature butter
1¾ cups sugar
3 eggs
2 tsp. vanilla
2¾ cups flour
3 tsp. baking powder
1 tsp. salt
1¼ cups milk

Preheat oven to 350°. (If baking cupcakes, preheat oven to 400° and prepare cupcake pans for 2 dozen.) Grease and lightly flour two 9-inch cake pans or one 13 x 9-inch cake pan.

In a large mixing bowl (use either a stand mixer or hand mixer) mix the butter, sugar, eggs, and vanilla. Beat this until super fluffy, at least 5 minutes on high speed. Trust me on this part—it makes all the difference in the texture.

While the mixer is doing its thing, sift your flour. In another medium-sized bowl, stir together the sifted flour, baking powder, and salt.

Turn your mixer to low and alternate adding in small amounts of the milk and dry ingredients, adding about a third of each at a time. Continue mixing until fully combined and then pour batter into prepared pans.

- Bake 9-inch cakes for 35 to 40 minutes.
- Bake oblong cake for 45 to 50 minutes.
- Bake cupcakes for 18 to 20 minutes.

To check if cake is done, insert a toothpick in the center. If it comes out clean, take the cakes out of the oven. Let cool in pan for 10 minutes. After 10 minutes, run a knife between the edge of the pan and the cake, turn upside down onto wire racks, and allow to cool completely. Frost when completely cooled.

Buttercream Frosting

½ cup softened butter
3 cups powdered sugar
Pinch of salt
1½ tsp. vanilla
2 to 3 T. cream

In a large mixing bowl, use a stand mixer or hand electric mixer and beat softened butter until light and creamy. Add in sugar, salt, and vanilla. Cream together on low until fully incorporated. Thin with cream, starting with 1 tablespoon at a time until it reaches desired consistency.

Variations:

- *Lemon frosting*: Omit vanilla and use lemon juice in place of the cream.
- *Chocolate frosting*: Use 2½ cups powdered sugar and ½ cup cocoa powder.

Chocolate Depression-Era Crazy Cake

Need a chocolate cake? The answer is yes, one always needs a chocolate cake. This cake originated in the Great Depression, when eggs, butter, and dairy were scarce. It goes by a few names, both as Wacky Cake or Crazy Cake.

In ode to my great-grandmother, I use some cold coffee, which is known to heighten the flavor of chocolate in baked goods. You can omit it if you like, but I never bake a chocolate cake without it.

You can double this to make a layered cake or a 13 x 9-inch sheet cake.

> 1½ cups flour
> 1 cup white sugar
> ¼ cup cocoa powder
> 1 tsp. baking soda
> ½ tsp. salt
> 1 tsp. vanilla extract
> 1 tsp. vinegar
> 6 T. oil (melted lard, coconut oil, or avocado oil would
>   be my picks)
> ½ cup cold water
> ½ cup cold coffee

Preheat oven to 350°. Mix together dry ingredients in a mixing bowl until well combined.

Tradition has you make 3 wells (holes) in the dry ingredients. Pour the vanilla in one hole, vinegar in one hole, and oil in the third hole.

Now pour the cold water and brewed coffee over the entire thing and stir until just combined.

Pour into an ungreased 8 x 8 pan and bake for 30 to 40 minutes, or until a toothpick in the center comes out clean. When cool, frost with topping of your choice!

* * *

After the candles are blown out, the last of the crumbs eaten, and the children are in bed, I have a special tradition that is as much for me as it is for them.

I pull out their baby books and remember back to the moment they entered the world. From the first sound of their cry to the way they took my breath away with a fierce love I'd never known before.

Every year I write them a letter. I share funny or cherished memories from the past 365 days, what they're learning, and what they mean to me. It's my place for me to tell them my hopes, prayers, and dreams for them for the coming year and the rest of their life. Then I tuck this letter into their baby book to give them someday when they're grown.

This can be done with grown children, small children, grandkids, or any special person in your life.

Thanksgiving

Thanksgiving is one of my favorite holidays. I love the focus of gratitude, family, and let's be honest, the good eats.

There's a part of me that really adores cooking a huge meal and having leftovers for days. Say I'm not the only one?

I've learned to bake my pies the day before, if possible, to have plenty of oven space for the bird. I usually make my pie crusts up a few weeks ahead of time and freeze them. Like many of you, I work the day before Thanksgiving at my day job, so having the pie crusts and pies done ahead of time helps to lighten the load. After all, the whole point of Thanksgiving is to be thankful—not stressed out and overwhelmed.

We also have a potluck strategy in our family. Everyone brings at least one or two dishes to help out the host. Everyone in our family welcomes this policy, especially because we rotate who is the host every year.

If we're hosting, of course we roast a big old turkey, but even if we have the meal elsewhere, I still roast a turkey for us.

Roasted Turkey

Whole turkey
1 to 2 onions
4 cloves garlic
3 sprigs fresh rosemary
4 to 5 leaves fresh sage
Salt
Pepper
¼ cup butter

To prepare the bird, thaw it out in the fridge at least 2 days ahead of time if frozen (3 if it's a large bird).

Preheat oven to 325° and get out your roasting pan and rack.

Remove the giblets, neck, and gravy packet (because we're going to make real gravy). Rinse the inside and out of the birdie; dry well.

Peel the onion and cut into thick wedges. Peel and crush cloves of garlic to release the oils. Sprinkle the inside of the bird with sea salt. Stuff the cavity with onions, garlic, and fresh rosemary and sage.

Using kitchen twine, truss your turkey by tying the legs closed and wrapping around the tail.

Rub the butter all over the outside of the turkey. Sprinkle with sea salt and pepper. Place the bird *breast-side-down* in the rack and roasting pan. Turn breast-side-up the last quarter of the cooking time. A pair of cooking tongs is helpful with the turning, and an extra pair of hands to hold the pan in place, with oven mitts, of course. This keeps the breast from drying out and eliminates the need for aluminum foil.

Cook in preheated oven according to weight and time.

Weight	Cook-Time (Unstuffed)
5-7 lbs.	2-2½ hrs.
7-9 lbs.	2½-3 hrs.

9-18 lbs.	3-3½ hrs.
18-22 lbs.	3½-4 hrs.
22-24 lbs.	4-4½ hrs.

Turkey is done when the internal temperature is 180° in the thigh and 165° in the breast. Make sure the thermometer is not touching the bone.

Place the turkey onto a platter and let it rest for 15 minutes before carving to retain the juices.

Turkey Gravy

After you've put the turkey to rest on the platter, strain out the liquid from the bottom of the pan, and place your roasting pan over two burners on the stove on medium-high heat.

Add ¼ cup flour to the drippings and stir to create a thin paste. When this begins to bubble, whisk while pouring in 1 to 2 cups strained broth, water, or milk. Start with 1 cup and whisk the whole time. If it's too thick, add an additional cup. Allow it to cook for a couple of minutes to thicken up, if needed.

Season with salt and pepper to taste.

Roast Carrots

I think carrots are an underappreciated vegetable. They're so versatile, but they rarely get to shine in cookbooks or at the table. They add gorgeous color when grated finely on top of a salad or added to soup. I have two picky eaters in my home who think they don't like carrots, but they never notice when I grate them into sauces or soups.

One of my favorite treats is roasted carrots. I've been known to eat an entire pan by myself. I'm a bit of a purist with my roasted carrots, whereas my mother prefers hers candied, with butter and brown sugar. Either way, they're a frugal addition to the kitchen, from a side dish to stretching out the soup and sauces...and feeding unexpected guests.

½ lb. carrots, rinsed, peeled, and chopped
2 T. coconut oil or butter
Sea salt to taste
2 T. brown sugar (optional)
Cinnamon to taste (optional)

Preheat oven to 375°. Place carrots in a covered baking dish, dot the tops with coconut oil or butter, and sprinkle with salt (for candied option, add sugar and spice). Bake for 20 minutes or until carrots are tender.

Pumpkin Puree

One of my favorite things about autumn is the pumpkins. Often-times, the sugar pie pumpkins will hide under the leaves of the vine, and it's not until they ripen I'll see a bit of orange peeking out at me. They decorate the garden before they come inside to decorate the house.

When you harvest pumpkins, wipe down the outside with a vinegar-moistened towel. This will help remove any bacteria on the outside that would break it down faster. Our pumpkins will last for a couple months on open shelving or front and center on the kitchen table as a centerpiece.

Not only do they make fabulous decorations, but they provide a special treat when they give up their seeds. For baking purposes, a sugar or pie pumpkin has the best flavor and is naturally sweeter. These are the smaller pumpkins, not the large ones for carving.

We never buy pumpkin pie filling or pureed pumpkin. It's very simple to do at home and much cheaper. Take your pumpkin and a sharp knife. Pop off the stem (or cut if it's still a bit green) and chop the pumpkin in half. Careful—they tend to roll a bit.

Scoop out the seeds and the stringy flesh parts clinging to the seeds (save the seeds to roast and snack on later) and place each half of the pumpkin cut side down in a 9 × 13-inch baking pan with an inch of water and bake at 375° for about 30 to 40 minutes (depending upon the size of your pumpkin), or until pumpkin is soft and fully cooked.

Remove pan from oven and allow to cool. Scoop out the soft pumpkin flesh. I use the edge of a large spoon and scrape it off the skin. Place cooked pumpkin into a blender or food processor (you can go old-school and use a potato masher too) and puree that baby up. Usually the sugar or pie pumpkins have drier flesh, which means more flavor, so you don't need to strain it. You may need to add a teensy bit of water if it's too dry, but just a tablespoon or so.

Look at you, you just made pumpkin puree and it tastes so much better than the tin can stuff at the store. You can use it to bake with immediately, store it in the fridge for up to 5 to 7 days, or pop it in the freezer for later.

Pumpkin puree or pie filling is *not* a candidate for home canning as it's too thick, even in a pressure canner, for the heat to penetrate through and kill all the botulism spores. Commercial pressure canners can reach higher temperatures than home ones.

When freezing, I like to freeze mine in either 1- or 2-cup portions for ease when baking. You can freeze it in a plastic freezer bag or my favorite, a pint-size Mason jar.

Now let's get our cookie making on!

Pumpkin Sugar Cookies

It took me about 3 times to get this recipe just right as I didn't want a pumpkin cookie that was really a muffin top in disguise. I wanted an honest-to-goodness cookie. Depending upon your palate, you can use either the smaller or larger amounts of spices indicated. Go ahead, make it your own.

½ cup melted butter
¼ cup coconut oil

½ cup brown sugar
½ cup white sugar
1 T. molasses
1 cup cooked pumpkin
2 cups all-purpose flour
1 tsp. baking powder
½ tsp. salt
2 tsp. ground cinnamon
½ to 1 tsp. ground nutmeg
½ to 1 tsp. ground ginger

Melt the butter and then add the coconut oil to the melted butter. The heat from the melted butter will soften up the coconut oil. In a large mixing bowl, cream together the melted butter, coconut oil, brown and white sugars, and molasses. Then add in and combine the cooked pumpkin.

Dump in all your dry ingredients and mix until combined. Cover and allow dough to chill in the fridge for at least an hour or even overnight. Trust me on this part. Chilled dough makes better flavored and textured cookies. Something magical happens upon chilling and all the flavors mingle together.

Preheat oven to 375°.

You have two options after your dough has chilled:

Option 1

For a puffier pumpkin sugar cookie, place some sugar in a bowl and roll a good-sized tablespoon of dough (use an ice cream scoop to easily create uniform cookies) into a ball and then roll it around in the sugar until it's fully coated. Place 2 inches apart on a cookie sheet and bake for 8 to 10 minutes, just until cookie has set. Allow cookies to cool for 5 minutes before removing from sheet.

Option 2

For a flatter, but still perfectly soft pumpkin sugar cookie, take a heaping tablespoon of dough and plop it on your cookie sheet. With your fingers, flatten it out into the desired size of your cookie, about a quarter-inch thick. The cookies will only slightly spread out as they bake. Sprinkle a light dusting of sugar on top of each cookie. Bake for 8 to 10 minutes, just until the cookies have set. Allow cookies to cool for 5 minutes before removing from sheet.

Grandma's Pumpkin Roll

This next dish is one of our favorite ways to serve pumpkin. It comes from my husband's grandmother's kitchen. Grandma gave me a lesson on how to make it, because I don't know about your house, but it seems no matter what, no one makes it as good as Grandma (even if I have her recipe) so I wanted to take notes and have a hands-on lesson.

One of the beautiful things about this recipe is you can bake it ahead of time and freeze it. Then in the mad dash of the holiday, you don't have to worry about preparing dessert. My husband's grandmother is quite renowned for her pumpkin rolls—in fact, I have a hunch she could make these year-round and have a bona fide home business. But lucky for you and me, she shared her recipe.

Cake Mixture

- ¾ cup flour
- 1 tsp. baking powder
- ½ tsp. salt
- ½ tsp. ground nutmeg
- 1½ tsp. ground cinnamon
- ½ tsp. ground ginger
- 3 eggs, well beaten until light and foamy
- 1 cup sugar
- ⅔ cup cooked pumpkin

Filling

- 1 cup powdered sugar (plus more for sprinkling)
- 8 ounces cream cheese
- ½ cup butter, softened
- 1 tsp. vanilla extract
- 2 tsp. maple syrup (optional)

Preheat oven to 375°. Grease and flour a 15 x 10-inch jelly roll pan with coconut oil—be generous with your grease.

Mix together flour, baking powder, salt, and spices. In a large mixing bowl, beat eggs for 5 minutes (yes, the whole 5 minutes) until light and foamy; cream in sugar and cooked pumpkin. Then stir in dry ingredients and stir until combined.

Pour into prepared jelly roll pan and spread until even. Pick up the pan and tap it (the bottom of the pan) against the counter a few times, this makes the air bubbles rise up out of the batter. (I jumped when Grandma did this. It makes a bang.)

Bake for 13 to 15 minutes, until cake is done. Place a clean flour sack or tea towel on the counter and sprinkle with a bit of powdered sugar.

As soon as the cake comes out of the oven, run a butter knife around the outside edge of the cake to separate it from the pan. Immediately, using hot pads, turn the pan upside down over the prepared towel.

As soon as cake is out of the pan, place another clean flour sack towel on the short end of the cake and roll up like a sleeping bag. Cool on a wire rack for about 30 minutes.

Prepare your filling by creaming together all of the filling ingredients. Unroll cooled cake and spread the filling evenly over the surface. Reroll the cake, cover, and allow to chill in fridge. Before serving, sprinkle with powdered sugar if desired.

Leftovers

Is it just me, or do we all need a bit of inspiration for that leftover turkey after Thanksgiving? This past year the smallest turkey I could find (we aren't raising our own turkeys...yet) was a 20-pound bird. We didn't host a big Thanksgiving party, so needless to say, I had mounds of leftover turkey. The dishes below were born of necessity—needing to whip something up for dinner and not wanting any of the leftovers to go to waste.

Turkey Skillet Supper

> 1 cup wild rice (quinoa would work too)
> 2 T. olive oil
> 1 clove garlic, minced
> 2 T. onion, diced
> 1 cup frozen peas (or use canned, drained peas)
> 2 T. water
> Salt and pepper
> 2 cups cubed cooked turkey
> 2 cups brown gravy
> ½ cup milk

Cook the wild rice (or your favorite rice or substitute) according to package directions. Start this first so it will be finished right when the rest of the dish is.

Place a large skillet on medium heat and add olive oil. When oil is warm toss in the garlic and onions and sauté for a minute. Next add the frozen peas and water. Cook until peas are hot, about 4 to 5 minutes. Season with a dash of salt and pepper.

Add in the cooked cubed turkey and gravy. Stir until gravy begins to melt and coat everything. Thin with the milk to create a sauce, stirring until the milk is incorporated with the gravy. Serve over cooked rice.

White Turkey Chili

Now don't get me wrong, I love me some turkey and dumplings, but I needed something a tad bit different on the palate come the sixth night of turning turkey into our supper.

The dried and shelled beans from this year's garden were still sitting in the colander waiting to go in Mason jars for next year's planting and for eating through the winter. That's when my inspiration hit and I popped this chili together.

Normally, I do a cold soak on my dried beans, where I put them in cold water and let them soak for 18 to 24 hours. However, in the busyness of the week, I forgot to soak them the night before.

Thankfully, you can also do a hot soak method when you're running short on time. Put your beans in a large pot and completely cover with water by a couple of inches. Bring to a boil and let boil for 3 minutes. Put the lid on, turn off the heat, and let sit for 1 to 4 hours.

Drain the beans, rinsing thoroughly in cold water. Place them back in your pot, cover with water, and simmer for 1½ to 2 hours, or until tender. Don't add salt until the end, as salt can result in a tough bean.

3 cups dried beans,
  prepared via cold or hot soak method
1 cup onion, diced
8 cloves garlic, minced
2 cups cooked turkey, diced
1 jalapeno, seeded and minced
1 T. chili powder
2 tsp. ground cumin
2 tsp. sea salt
1 tsp. garlic powder
1 tsp. onion powder
Fresh ground black pepper to taste

After soaking your beans via either method, drain them and then place them in a large soup pot. Cover with fresh, cold water by 2 inches. Bring to a boil. Allow to simmer, stirring occasionally, for 1 hour.

Add the onion, garlic, and jalapeno pepper. Let simmer for another half hour. Add water a half cup at a time if the soup becomes too thick.

When beans are tender and vegetables are cooked, stir in the turkey and seasonings. Continue to cook until turkey is heated, about 5 to 10 minutes, and serve.

This is excellent topped with a bit of grated cheese and a dollop of sour cream or yogurt.

Christmas

I love lanterns and oil lamps. I have an oil lamp sitting on the counter in our kitchen for both decorative purposes and so it's handy when the power goes out. One of the oldest and simplest light forms that is still in use in many homes today, regardless of electricity or not, is the humble candle.

It doesn't matter how dark a room is, the smallest flame from a candle will push back the night.

I keep a candle in just about every room of the house. When the power goes out, I know I've got a light source until I can get our larger oil lamp lit.

They're also a daily reminder of how the power of Jesus works. It doesn't matter how big and dark our sin is or how much of a mess we've made of our lives, once we allow the flame of His love and salvation to light in our soul, it eliminates the dark.

The laws of nature follow the laws of the cross. You can have a candle lit in a sunny room and as night falls, the shadows will begin to encroach, growing larger as the earth spins. But unless that candle burns out, even at the height of midnight, that darkness can never snuff out that flame. And if you give that candle more fuel, it will burn brighter and brighter, pushing back the dark.

That is the beauty of a life lived with Jesus in our heart and serving

Him. As we grow in Him, our light burns brighter, chasing away the dark.

> Neither do people light a lamp and put it under a bowl. Instead they put it on its stand, and it gives light to everyone in the house (Matthew 5:15).

A pioneer Christmas was much more frugal than our modern ones, but every bit as special. Isn't that the key to this old-fashioned life, finding out that spending less doesn't mean actually having less, but really having more of what's important?

One of my favorite odes to the people of old is making homemade gifts. Sometimes I'll purchase something from the store to go with it, create a whole basket of homemade items, or even give just one homemade candle or jar of jam.

My kids will often help in the creation, and this is a great bonding time for us. Plus, it teaches them valuable skill sets, not only in the how-to but also in the heart, to create something with someone else in mind.

Below you'll find tutorials and instructions for crafting homemade gifts, but you'll also want to include some of the items from chapter 4. Here are some ideas to get you started:

- For the chef, baker, or foodie in your life, create a basket of all the homemade spice mixes.

- For a spa basket with natural goodness for soul and mind fill with the Epsom bath salts, Peppermint Chocolate Body Lotion, a Beeswax Candle (see recipe below), and a bar of your homemade soap.

- For natural health–minded folks, how about a bottle of homemade tincture, herbal tea blend, and the Skin-Soothing Salve.

Beeswax Candles

Not only are candles a simple light source and a good visual reminder of the power of God, but they're also simple to make at home.

Many of the candles you buy in the store have chemicals and toxic pollutants in them, which fill our homes and air. They might smell good, but we don't see the invisible vapors being released into our homes.

When we look back to the days of old, we see that candles were frequently used. One of the beauties of a candle is they can be made easily at home using ingredients one could produce off of their own land if needed.

While there are many waxes available, I wanted my homemade candles to be made from natural ingredients. Almost any fat source will burn, though some aren't going to smell very nice, and though we're after function, a pleasant end product is also a plus.

Beeswax is our first ingredient. If you have honeybee hives, you'll be able to harvest your own beeswax. However, most of us aren't bee keepers. You can purchase beeswax online from various retailers, in craft stores, and often co-ops or health food stores. I'm lucky enough to have two local bee keepers in our area and can purchase beeswax from them.

If you purchase beeswax from a store, beeswax sold in pellet form is the easiest for measuring and melting quickly. Beeswax from a local beekeeper will come in larger hard blocks. You can chop small chunks off with a knife. I've also tried grating it and it works somewhat. Another option is to melt the beeswax over a double boiler and pour it into smaller molds for quick use later.

The next ingredient in our candles is a fat source. While beeswax will burn all by itself, it does burn hot. Adding in another fat source helps make a softer candle and helps keep the wax from cracking (because we want them to look pretty too, right?), and my two choices are lard and coconut oil. The pioneers of old often used tallow (beef fat) or lard to make candles, without the addition of other waxes. As much as I love our home-rendered lard for baking and cooking, I don't necessarily want to smell animal fat burning when I light my candles. The beeswax naturally smells of honey when it's heated. Score! In fact, when I was making up a batch recently, my husband came in and said, "That smells awesome."

Beeswax is hard when cooled, but turns to liquid when heated. If beeswax is melted at too high of a temperature, it can become discolored and also scorch or burn. This usually happens when it reaches a temperature of 185°. We want our beeswax to smell like honey when it's burning, not burned wax. To avoid all of this, you will want to melt the waxes and oils in a double boiler. If you don't have an official double boiler, they're easy to make—and what I always use. I don't like having to purchase something if I can use things I already have to get the job done.

Fill a saucepan with 2 inches of water. You'll need a smaller vessel, preferably either a metal pouring pot (they're shaped more like a pitcher as they have tall sides) or a Pyrex measuring cup or a Mason jar. I have a measuring cup and a Mason jar I leave as my dedicated wax/oil melting pots. That way I don't have to worry about cleaning out the melted and reset wax and oils.

The smaller container needs to be small enough that the water can surround the sides. You don't want the container actually touching the bottom of the pan, because then it's directly against the heat source. To avoid this, I put a few canning bands in the bottom of the pot to act as a shelf for my pouring pot. Works like a charm.

Bring the water to a boil then turn it down to a simmer—a gentle boil. Put your pot/jar with the measured beeswax down into the water. The smaller the chunks of beeswax, the faster it will melt. Stir occasionally using a metal spoon until all the beeswax is almost melted. Now add in your fat source, it will melt much quicker than the beeswax did. Once completely melted together, take off of heat. If you're adding in any essential oils or fragrance oils, now is the time do so. Stir it in along with your fat source. When everything is mixed together, pour your wax into the candle containers.

(Remember, if you ever do have beeswax or any other oil catch on fire in your kitchen, never, ever, try to put it out with water. This will only cause the fire to spread. You need to smother it—put a lid on the pot, or your surest bet is to use a fire extinguisher. I've never had this happen to me, but it's always best to be prepared ahead of time.)

Next up we need a wick source. Many store-bought candles use wicks with either lead or metal wire in the center. I don't know about you, but I don't really want the toxins from burning lead or metals floating around the air in my home. We use all cotton wicks, without any metals or lead.

Choosing the size of your wick will depend upon the diameter of the container you're using for your candle. A regular mouth Mason jar (from the inside of the jar, not the outer rim) is just past 1½ inches. They flare out a bit at the shoulder of the jar on the pint sizes to almost 2 inches.

I really like the smaller eight-ounce jelly jars for candles. The small-size natural paper wicks from Candle Science perform very nice in these jars for me. If you're using a larger diameter container, you'll likely want to go up in size on your wick (the size is not the length of the wick but the thickness of it).

You'll want to do a few test jars before making a large batch to make sure you have the correct wick size for your beeswax and container.

After candles have cured for at least 24 hours, trim the wick to ¼ inch length above the surface of the wax.

Light the candle and let it burn for 2 hours. At the end of the two hours the wax should be all the way (or fairly close) melted to the sides of the jar/container. If there is a lot of soot or mushrooming of the wick it's probably too big. On the other hand, if the melted wax isn't reaching out to the sides of the container, the wick may be too small.

Candle Size Guidelines

These are the guidelines I follow when testing out a new jar size for a candle. We don't want the full weight of the jar in wax as it would be too much. If you have an eight-ounce jar you don't want a total of eight ounces of wax/fat. I do three quarters of the total container capacity. For example, on an eight-ounce jar I would use six ounces of wax/fat. For a six-ounce jar I would use four and half ounces of wax/fat.

Then I break down the amount of beeswax to the amount of either coconut oil or lard. I use two thirds beeswax and one third fat. For the eight-ounce jars I use four ounces of beeswax and two ounces of fat. The largest jar size I've used to date is eight ounces.

Formula for amount of wax and fat per jar = ¾ of the total jar capacity

Formula for wax and fat ratio= ⅔ wax + ⅓ fat source

Candle Ingredients (For One Candle)

> **8-ounce glass jelly jar**
> **4 ounces beeswax**
> **2 ounces coconut oil or lard**
> **1 wick**
> **Wick centering device (optional)**

1. Center your wick. If you purchased wicks with adhesive tabs, then attach the wick base to the center of the jar. If not, use a hot glue gun and attach it to the center of the jar. Use a candle wick centering device to help center the wick

and to keep tension on the wick when pouring the wax and letting it cool. Note: You can also use a pencil: tape the end of the wick to the pencil and roll it until it's taut, with the pencil resting lengthwise across the top of the jar. However, you wouldn't want to put the pencil in the oven, so this step will need to be done right before pouring.

2. Preheat your oven to 170°. Put your jelly jars on a cookie sheet and place them in the oven to warm up. (The heat does melt the hot glue a bit, but I just push it down right before pouring and haven't had a problem.)

3. Heat up your double boiler. While the double boiler is heating, measure out the beeswax and fat into your melting container. When double boiler is boiling, adjust heat to a simmer and place your melting container inside. Stir occasionally and keep an eye on your melting waxes and fat. It will take about 20 to 30 minutes (depending upon the size of your beeswax chunks or pellets) to melt.

4. When wax is fully melted, remove melting container from the heat. Add in any fragrances if using and stir well to incorporate them. Many people only use essential oils so the scent is not synthetic, but beeswax doesn't throw scent (meaning the candles don't give a lot of scent when burning), and because the beeswax already smells like honey, I choose not to add the extra expense of fragrance. This is totally up to you!

5. With a hot pad or oven mitt (the jars aren't extremely hot at 170°, but I wouldn't grab them bare-handed), take your jars out of the oven and pour your candles. Turn off the oven.

6. Place candles back in the now-turned-off oven and allow to cool in the warm environment. When using this method of slowly cooling the wax, I haven't experienced any cracks in the finished candle. I did experiment with poking relief holes in the wax, but found it wasn't needed when letting cool in the warm oven, so now I skip the step of having to do a re-pour.

7. When candles are cooled to solid, remove from the oven and allow to cure for at least 24 hours. Trim the wick to ¼ inch above the surface of the candle and enjoy!

One note regarding clean up: I use a dedicated spoon and melting containers to avoid having to get all the wax out. But if you have a utensil that needs to be used for something else, pour just-off-the-boil water over it, then wipe clean with a paper towel you can throw away. You don't want beeswax water going through your pipes.

Soap

The pioneers of old made almost everything by hand. The sheer amount of knowledge these folks possessed is astounding. So much of what we purchase today was commonly made at home.

One of those items is soap. Back in the day, the pioneers made their own lye from wood ash and rendered the fat from their beef (tallow) and pigs (lard) to mix with it. Many people today still make soap with lye (you can't make soap without it) and fat, but they don't make their own lye; they purchase it from the store. Lye is caustic and needs to be used with care given to safety and proper procedure.

Always wear safety goggles, long-sleeved shirts, long pants, and rubber gloves when mixing your lye water and throughout the soap-making process. Use a room with good ventilation and make sure no small children or pets are present. Have vinegar on the counter, as it neutralizes lye.

For those just getting into soap making, one of the easiest ways to make soap is to use the melt-and-pour method. You purchase a base of lye and oils that's already been through the saponification process and is fully cured.

This means you get to use the soap sooner without the curing process and don't have to worry about getting ratios just right or having a failed batch. If you're wanting a project to use with the kids, this is a much safer route.

You can purchase the base in one- or two-pound increments or all the way up to ten or twenty pounds for making large batches.

This lets you create your own scents and colors (if you wish to add color powder), and though some of the work has been done for you, it's still much cheaper than purchasing a handmade bar of soap at the store or craft fair.

There are many options for the melt-and-pour bases including goat's milk, shea butter, clear, glycerin, and cocoa butter. Make sure to the check the ingredients list for soy or gluten. I prefer to use non-soy and GMO-free ingredients, even in our skin care. For the exact items I use, visit the Resource page at www.handmadethebook.com.

Melt-and-Pour Soap

Melt-and-Pour Base
Scale if using fragrance or essential oils
    and/or colorant
Thermometer

Additive Options:
- Essential Oils
(only use oils suitable for contact with the skin)

- Dried herbs (finely chopped)

- Oatmeal (finely chopped)

- Honey

Here's how to make melt-and-pour soap. You can simply double this if you have a two-pound melt-and-pour base.

Lemon Lime Soap

1 lb. (16 ounces) melt-and-pour Goat's Milk Soap Base
4.5 grams lime essential oil
3.5 grams lemon essential oil
½ tsp. dried zest of lime and lemon

Prepare your mold. You can purchase soap molds, line any suitably sized container with freezer paper, use silicone muffin cups, or line a bread pan with freezer paper. For a one-pound batch I use my 7 x 4 x 2-inch loaf pan.

Sprinkle the dried zest on the bottom of the prepared mold. Alternatively, you can mix the zest into the soap instead of just placing it in the mold.

Place two inches of water in the bottom of a saucepan with a canning band in the center and bring to a boil. Chop up the melt-and-pour base into even pieces and put in a melting container. A Pyrex measuring bowl or quart-sized Mason jar work well.

Turn the water down to a simmer and place your melting container filled with the chopped melt-and-pour base on top of the canning band, creating a shelf. Stir until the chunks of the melt-and-pour base are completely melted. Make sure it doesn't exceed 140° or it can burn. Remove from the heat and place on a hot pad.

Measure out your essential oils.

Let it cool down slightly before adding your scents—about 120° is preferred. As it cools, the top may form a film—just stir every 3 to 4 minutes to stir in the film. When the melted base has cooled to about 120°, add the essential oil.

Stir in desired scents and additives, mixing well together. Pour into prepared molds and allow to set and cool for 24 hours. Remove from molds and cut into bars if needed.

To cut bars, use a ruler and mark every 1 or 2 inches by making a score mark with a knife. I prefer a 1-inch bar of soap. Then use a sharp knife and slice at your measurements.

 I don't have decades of soap-making experience under my belt, but I have the next best thing. My mother makes her own soap, and one of my good friends, Julie, and her friend Karen, have been making their own soap together for more than 16 years. There is something to be said for years of experience, and I was super excited when Julie and Karen offered to give me some hands-on lessons and share their knowledge and expertise with you in this book.

 The beauty of homemade soap is being able to control the ingredients and scents that go into it. And let's be honest, being able to say you make your own soap is pretty awesome.

 There are a few methods of making soap, but they all contain lye. Melt-and-pour methods have already done the work for you, cold and hot process methods are when you mix the lye in yourself, but all true soap contains lye.

 The cold process requires curing time before being able to use the soap. We do use heat, but we don't "cook" the soap as long, and it does its curing during the cooling process, hence the cold method name.

 To start with, you're going to need some basic tools and ingredients.

Handmade Soap (Cold Process Method)

Large pot
Food scale
Lye
Oil/fat source
Distilled water
Two Pyrex or heat-safe measuring bowls for making
    the lye water
One large heat-safe bowl to measure the oils and fat
Plastic or silicone spatula
Large spoon
Vinegar
Safety goggles
Safety rubber gloves
Immersion blender
Essential oils (optional for scent)
Coloring powder (optional for color)
Soap mold
Freezer paper

Where to Purchase Your Ingredients

You used to be able to purchase lye at the grocery store, but many stores no longer carry it, as it was used to make illegal substances and can be dangerous if not handled properly. You can order lye online at soap making websites such as Brambleberry.com or Amazon. The lye (sodium hydroxide) is the type used for making solid bars of soap.

The recipe I'm sharing with you from Julie and Karen uses olive oil, palm oil, and coconut oil. You can use other oils, such as lard, tallow, or cocoa butter, just to name a few. Always start with a recipe from a reliable source when first starting out. As you become more comfortable and experienced, you may create your own recipes with the oils and fats you have on hand. You can find a Soap Calculator through an online search.

You'll need a scale to measure out your ingredients. This recipe is done in grams and creates 20 one-inch-thick bars of soap for a mold that is 3 x 20 inches long and 3.5 inches deep, or approximately a 6-pound batch.

Many soap makers prefer a wooden mold. Karen's father helped them make their molds, but you can also find wooden soap molds for sale online or in soap shops. My mother lines a shoe box with freezer paper or plastic wrap, and I've even used lined bread loaf pans. Get creative—as long as the container can be lined and will hold the full batch, use it!

Cold-Process Oatmeal Honey Soap

> 384 grams palm oil
> 439 grams coconut oil
> 576 grams olive oil
> 200 grams lye
> 462 grams distilled water
> ½ cup finely ground oatmeal (optional)
> 3 ounces warm honey (optional)
> ½ tsp. colorant powder (optional)
> 40 to 60 grams essential oil (optional)

1. Put the containers of palm and coconut oil in a sink or dishwashing tub full of hot water to melt the oils to liquid state.

2. Line the soap mold with the freezer paper. Leave the edges long so you can wrap it over and easily pull up when it's time to remove the soap.

3. Put on your safety glasses and gloves. Wear long sleeves and pants when working with lye and making soap.

4. Carefully measure the lye into one of the heat-safe bowls, preferably with a pour spout, and set aside. Measure the distilled water into a heat-safe bowl (when you add the lye it will get HOT). Put the measured distilled water on your stove top with *the exhaust fan on.*

5. Slowly (do not dump it all in at once) *pour the lye* into the distilled water. *Never* pour the water into the lye, it can cause an eruption of lye and cause dangerous burns.

6. Stir the lye into the water and stay at arm's length—you don't want to inhale the fumes. You'll see the fumes as the lye is mixed in. Stir until the lye is dissolved into the water. Make sure this is done in a well-ventilated area, not a small room, and preferably under an exhaust fan. It's not advised to have pets or small children running around during this time. Once the lye is completely dissolved in the water it will be 180°.

7. When the oils have started to melt enough to pour, turn on your scale and measure out your oils. Put a large pot on the stove over low heat and pour in the measured palm and coconut oil; continue stirring until the oils are fully melted, usually around 120° to 125°. Be sure the pot has been washed well, as any particles of food or other substances could contaminate your soap. **Safety Note:** It's advised to have dedicated soap making tools and utensils to avoid cross-contamination with your food or accidental ingestion of the lye.

8. Keep an eye on the temperature of our oil and lye. They both need to cool down to 90° in order to mix the lye with the oils. Place the container with the lye mixture in the sink in a small amount of cold water.

9. It's much faster and easier to use an infrared (point and shoot) thermometer. If you're relying on a regular cooking or candy thermometer, you'll want to use two. Otherwise when going back and forth between the oil and the lye, you'll have to thoroughly wash, rinse, and dry it every single time (see, just get the infrared).

10. Pour the olive oil into the other oils to help cool it down faster. Usually the addition of the olive oil will drop it by approximately 20°. When both the lye and the oil are cooled to 90° (it's more important for the two of them to be the same temperature rather than exactly 90°), slowly pour the lye into the oils while constantly stirring the oils with the immersion blender, but do not turn on the blender yet, just use it as a spoon. Don't stir directly into the stream of the lye, but try to cover the entire pot.

11. Once all the lye is poured in, continue stirring with the immersion blender, only pulsing it with the blender every 30 seconds or so. If you use the blender continually you'll reach the tracing point too soon and it will also introduce air pockets. Don't stop stirring, though, or your soap might not set.

12. The soap will begin to turn a creamy color and thicken up. Continue stirring and pulsing until it reaches the trace. The tracing point is when it becomes thick like pudding and if you drizzle some of the liquid over the top, it will form a line on top before dissolving back into the rest of the soap (see in photo below). This generally takes about 5 minutes.

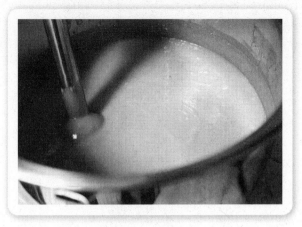

13. Once it's reached the trace, stir in any scents, colorants, or other items you're using in the soap. For honey oatmeal soap, pour in the finely ground ½ cup oatmeal and stir—you don't want any large clumps. Stir in honey and mix until combined well. The honey oatmeal soap makes a great exfoliator and doesn't require any added scents.

14. Pour into your prepared soap mold. Cover the top of the soap with the flap of wax or freezer paper and put the lid on. Take a couple of thick towels or blankets and wrap the soap mold to keep the soap from cooling off too quickly during the next 24 hours. Try not to disturb it for the next 24 hours either.

15. After a few days, the soap will be set enough to cut into bars. Cut the bars and spread them out on a surface to allow them to finish curing. The curing process will take a total of 4 to 6 weeks to finish the saponification. At the end of the curing process there won't be any active lye left.

Saponification is the process of the lye (an alkali ingredient) and fat or oil (your acidic ingredient) creating a chemical reaction that produces soap and glycerin. The wonderful thing about handmade soap is the glycerin isn't stripped out, leaving a softer soap that's more nourishing to the skin. This recipe is considered superfatted, which means there's enough fat in the recipe for extra fat to be present in the finished soap for more moisturizing.

Cleanup

Vinegar neutralizes the lye. Pour vinegar over the spoons, spatulas, and the immersion blender (after it's been unplugged of course), and then wash with hot soapy water, rinse, and let dry. Pour vinegar into the bowls and pots, swish it up all the sides, and then wash, rinse, and dry. You may wish to still wear gloves when washing out your utensils and pots.

Cinnamon Salt Dough Ornaments

Your homemade soaps and candles make great gifts. It's a wonderful thing to be able to give someone gifts made with your own two hands. There's something extra special about a homespun gift during the holiday season.

These ornaments make a lovely gift and a beautiful addition to your tree. Use the cheapest cinnamon you can find—these aren't for eating, just for color and scent.

1¼ cups flour
½ cup salt
¾ cup ground cinnamon
¾ cups warm water

Preheat oven to 275°. In a mixing bowl thoroughly combine flour, salt, and cinnamon. Slowly stir in the warm water until it sticks together. Using your hands, knead the dough until it's soft enough to roll out—this also helps the salt to be evenly distributed through the dough to avoid white pockets in the finished ornaments. You may add a bit more water if needed, but you don't want this to be a wet dough.

For easiest rolling, place the dough directly on your cookie sheet and roll out to ⅛-inch thick. If you go thicker, the cookies will puff up and tend to cook unevenly.

Use your favorite cookie cutters to cut out your desired shapes. It's easiest if you leave the cut cookies on the cookie sheet and remove the extra dough from around them—we don't want to smoosh or rip off an arm from our gingerbread man, right?

Remember to use a straw or other item to create a large hole in the top of the ornament for a string or ribbon to hang it by.

You can use whole spices to decorate your ornaments just like regular cookies—think whole cloves or even star anise. If you want to create a pattern in the dough, do so now with a fork, stylist tool, rough weave burlap, or whatever texture you think would look awesome. I use the tines of a fork diagonally across the toe and heel of stocking shaped ornaments and along the cuff of mittens.

Bake for approximately 1 hour, until ornaments are hard. Your house will smell amazing.

Allow ornaments to cool. For a rustic look, use red, or red and white ribbon to hang on the tree.

Variation: If you don't want the cinnamon scent and the rustic brown color, omit the cinnamon and go with a full 2 cups of flour instead.

Want to let your artistic side flow?

Use acrylic paint to create a design and sprinkle the glitter on.

To create a shiny ornament, paint with a spray-on varnish or clear coat.

Yield: approximately 2 dozen 2 ½-inch ornaments

Canning Lid Christmas Ornaments

Don't toss out those used canning lids! Even though we can't use them to can again, they make great ornaments. I prefer the wide mouth lids because you have a slightly larger surface area to work with.

Paint your lids with two to three coats of paint (chalkboard or clay paint is my choice—it covers great and is safe to use indoors without fumes), allowing them to dry between coats. Your options are limitless and you can get as creative as you want.

I used hot glue to adhere the jute twine and ribbon to the top of the back of the lid to hang them by. Make sure your loop is large enough for your tree branches.

Rubber stamps are awesome when you're not that great of an artist or freehand painter. Hand raised!

A true homesteader, I headed back out to the yard and gathered up some of the chickens' feathers from this year's molting. Those girls are good for more than just eggs, my friend!

If you want to apply glitter, sprinkle it on when the paint is still wet.

A few other ideas:

- Use some small buttons (because you took my Great

Depression–Era Tip from earlier and started saving those, right?) for a snow man.

- A monogrammed style initial
- A favorite saying or verse. You can try this freehand, or else print it out on tracing paper in your favorite font and then trace over it.

Christmas Potpourri

One of the beautiful things about Christmas is the scents. The bright note of fresh cut pine with the spices of cinnamon, and you can practically see gingerbread dancing in the air.

However, as you might have guessed, I'm not a fan of synthetic fragrances, and neither is your pocketbook or your body. Great news, here's a simple and easy way to have your home smelling like Christmas.

1 to 2 sprigs fresh cut pine branches
2 to 4 cinnamon sticks
Slices of orange
1 to 2 tsp. cloves

Place all ingredients in a small to medium saucepan and completely cover with water. Allow to simmer on low to scent your home, adding water as needed to keep it from going dry. This can be done on a woodstove or regular stove, as well as in your slow cooker.

Easy Festive Holiday Decor

One of my favorite easy ways to decorate is to use fresh cedar or pine boughs. If you have trees on your property, go ahead and snip a few. If not, check with fresh Christmas tree lots. Often they trim the trees to make them more appealing.

Fill a Mason jar or vase with the branches. You can hang small ornaments off them, a string of popcorn, or even a small strand of lights. Their scent fills the air and lends an easy festive feel to any corner of the house.

One of my favorite centerpieces is to take three Mason jars of varying sizes and display them with candles inside—small votives, tea lights, pillar candles, or your homemade beeswax candles. You can also fill one of these jars with small ornaments. I have vintage light blue ornaments that I like to mix with white and silver ornaments, especially with the older blue Mason jars. Scatter some of the ornaments around the base of the jars.

Old-Fashioned Christmas Fudge

Some foods just say Christmas. Homemade old-fashioned fudge is one of those. Chocolate fudge is a Christmas and New Year's tradition at our home. Let me clarify, the eating of it on those days is tradition. But to save time and stress around the holidays, which can run a tad high, I'm about to let you in on some secrets I've learned.

Many a confectioner has been plagued with grainy fudge. Fudge should be light and creamy, not resembling the texture of sand. When I first set about making cooked fudge, I wanted to find out why some fudge turns out perfect and other batches have the dreaded grainy factor. I should have known my older cookbooks would contain the knowledge.

If you can get your hand on cookbooks published in the 1940s or earlier, they carry a treasure trove of lost advice and tips that are lacking in many modern cookbooks (which is one of the things I hope this book helps remedy for you). Some of the tips below come from a 1944 copy of *The Good Housekeeping Cook Book*.

1. Make sure you're using a heavy-bottomed saucepan. This will help keep your fudge from burning.

2. Take a stick of cold butter and grease the inside of the saucepan, making sure to coat the bottom and up the sides of the pot. This will help keep the fudge from sticking to the pan as much.

3. Follow the instructions exactly to ensure a creamy end product, this isn't the place to "fudge" the directions.

4. Stir the mixture constantly when first heating the fudge (this helps the milk not curdle), but once it reaches a boil, do not stir it. I repeat, DO NOT stir your fudge once it boils, ever. Unless you like grainy sand-textured fudge.

5. Always take a clean spoon (or rinse off and dry the same one) before allowing it to touch the fudge. Even a few grains of sugar on the spoon entered at the wrong time can cause a chain reaction and create the infamous grit factor to your fudge.

6. After taking the fudge off the heat, do not stir it until it has cooled down to 110°, or lukewarm to the touch. Once it's cooled, make sure you beat in the butter until it's no longer glossy before pouring into your prepared pan.

7. Don't scrape the side of the pan when beating or pouring out the fudge. I know, it will seem wrong to leave some of that delicious chocolate fudge clinging to the sides of the pot, but leave it, or you might cause that fudge to "sugar" and turn grainy.

Many fudge recipes call for the addition of corn syrup. It helps create a creamier texture, but with almost all the corn crops in the United States being genetically modified, I choose not to use it. You can search out an organic or certified GMO-free brand, but I haven't stocked it in our home for years. One less ingredient to purchase, the better in my opinion. I use honey instead.

You'll also find this fudge recipe calls for cocoa powder instead of unsweetened chocolate squares. I use cocoa powder in many different recipes and again, stocking one less ingredient helps keep my budget and supplies down.

2 cups sugar (evaporated cane juice works well)
⅓ cup cocoa powder
½ tsp. salt
1½ T. butter
1 cup milk (or water, though milk is standard)
2 T. honey
2 T. butter (I use salted)
1 tsp. vanilla extract

Butter your saucepan by smearing a cold stick of butter all over the bottom and lower parts of the side. Pour in sugar, cocoa powder, and salt; combine the dry ingredients until mixed. Add in the milk and honey and stir over low heat until sugar and cocoa are dissolved into the liquid. Occasionally scrape the bottom and the sides of the pan; once everything is incorporated, increase the heat a smidge, staying in the medium-low range, and stir constantly until the mixture reaches a boil.

As soon as it begins to boil, stop stirring. Allow to boil gently until fudge reaches 240°, also known as soft ball stage. (It takes 15 minutes on my stove once the mixture reaches a boil, but generally 12 to 15 minutes is suggested.)

It's normal for the fudge to foam up and climb up the sides of the pan as it boils. Resist the urge to stir it down. If you're close to foaming over, turn the heat down a little bit and *don't stir*. As it reaches closer to the soft ball stage temperature, it will begin to recede back down the sides of the pot.

Use a candy thermometer or the old-fashioned candy-making cold water test (see page 239). Because candy thermometers can sometimes be off by a few degrees or more, I prefer to use it as a guideline to tell me when I'm close to reaching temperature and confirm it by the soft ball stage test.

Once fudge reaches the soft ball stage, immediately remove it from the heat, but do so gently; try not to knock the pan too much. Place 2 tablespoons of butter on the top of the hot fudge; resist the urge to stir. Let it cool about an hour until it reaches 110°, or the fudge is lukewarm to the touch.

Once it's cooled, add 1 teaspoon vanilla extract and beat the butter and vanilla into the fudge until it loses its glossiness, for about 4 to 5 minutes.

Either grease or line your pan with parchment paper and pour fudge into it. This will make either an 8 x 8-inch square pan or a 9 x 5 x 3-inch loaf pan. Remember, don't scrape the sides of the pan clean to avoid sugaring.

Let fudge cool fully and then cut into squares. Store it in an airtight container or wrap it tightly; it will keep for up to 10 days in the fridge...if it lasts that long, which isn't likely due to its fabulousness.

Fudge can be made weeks or even a few months ahead and frozen in the freezer. I learned this tip from a sweet lady in the town where I work. She brought me in a plate, and I thought it was fresh; it was only afterward she told me it had been frozen and thawed. It thaws out beautifully and you can have your candy making done early!

I happen to be a purist when it comes to my chocolate fudge— I don't want any nuts. But I realize not everyone has my finicky taste buds, so if you like nuts in your fudge, finely chop ½ cup of your favorite nuts and add in with the vanilla.

How to Save Dry, Gritty Fudge

Even with following all the directions, something happened to your fudge. It's either powdery dry, or the dreaded sand in the mouth has happened. I can't stand the thought of throwing out all those ingredients.

You can salvage it by melting it back down and recooking it to the softball stage again. And you do this with a surprising ingredient: Water.

It seems contrary, like the water would make the chocolate seize, and the first time I tried it I fully expected it to fail. But it works.

Place your fudge in a saucepan with 1¼ cups of water (for a regular batch of fudge that fills an 8 x 8-inch pan or 9 x 5 x 3-inch loaf pan). Over medium-low heat, stir and melt the fudge until it is dissolved fully into the water. Then gently increase the heat to bring it to a boil. Don't stir once it's reached a boil. Cook until it reaches 240°, or soft ball candy stage via the cold water test.

Remove from heat, try not to shake or bump it, and let cool to 110° or lukewarm. Beat or stir until no longer glossy for 5 minutes and pour into a greased or parchment paper-lined pan.

Enjoy that now-creamy fudge you just saved!

The Soft-Ball Test

Fill a small, shallow glass bowl with cold water. Take a tablespoon of the boiling fudge and drop it into the cold water. If the candy isn't near soft ball stage, it will simply dissolve into the water.

Let it sit for a few seconds, and then reach your fingers into the water (the candy will sink to the bottom of the water) and scoop out the fudge. You should be able to roll it into a ball between your fingers and have it hold its shape, but it should remain malleable and you can still squish it.

If the chocolate dissolves in the water or won't hold the ball shape, it needs to boil for a few more minutes. If you can't squish the ball, you've cooked it too long. It's better to test early rather than too late.

To retest, dump out the water and place clean cold water in the bowl. Make sure you wash your spoon and thoroughly dry it before putting it back into the boiling fudge to test each time.

Soft Molasses Sugar Cookies

One of my best tips for Christmas baking, especially when it comes to pie crusts and cookie dough, is to make the dough up ahead of time. With hectic schedules and the busyness of the season, you may feel you can't find enough time to put in a full-on baking schedule. There's a reason those convenience tubes of dough in the store refrigerator and freezer sections sell. But you can make your own convenience for way less money and without the side addition of unsavory ingredients.

But the real reason, the real reason, my friends, is chilled cookie dough does something magical to the flavors and texture of your cookies. A few hours is better than nothing, but if you can go a full 24 hours or even pop it in the freezer for a few weeks, oh my. The flavors have a chance to really get to know one another, especially in spiced cookies. The fat content, be it butter or coconut oil, becomes firmer (wish the cold did that to me) and the structure and texture of the cookie is always improved.

Usually I can't wait to bake some of the cookies, so I'll bake one pan right when I make the dough and then freeze the other half of the dough for later. The frozen dough always turns out a better cookie.

Along with a small plate of fudge, we like to give a plate of our favorite homemade cookies to neighbors and friends...and to keep a small assortment at home to indulge in.

Some of my favorite Christmas cookies involve molasses. If we look back to the farms and homesteads of old, we find many recipes included molasses. One of the reasons is regular white sugar was expensive and hard to come by. For all my Laura Ingalls Wilder fans, you'll remember Ma put out the small amount of white sugar they had only when guests came.

This recipe first came to me via a customer at the pharmacy I worked in years ago. She brought us a plate of Christmas cookies, and the next time she came in I made sure to ask her for the recipe. They melt on your tongue, and you may hear the faint whisper of jingle bells while eating them. If I could make only one Christmas cookie a year, they'd be it. Thank goodness we're not limited to just one.

Many people have tried this recipe, and it's quickly become their cookie as well, which I hope will be the case for you.

> ¾ **cup softened butter**
> ½ **cup sugar (evaporated cane juice works fine)**
> ½ **cup brown sugar**
> ¼ **cup molasses (blackstrap is what we use)**
> **1 egg**
> **2 cups flour (all purpose or a blend of whole wheat**
>   **pastry and spelt work, too)**
> **2 tsp. baking soda**
> ½ **tsp. salt**
> **1 tsp. cinnamon**
> ½ **tsp. ginger**
> ½ **tsp. nutmeg**

In a large bowl, beat together the butter and sugars until creamy. Add molasses and egg, beating until well blended. In medium bowl, blend flour, soda, salt, cinnamon, ginger, and nutmeg; add to molasses mixture and mix well.

Cover and chill at least 20 minutes.

Form dough into 1-inch balls. To make uniform balls that bake evenly, use an ice cream scoop. Roll each in sugar and place 2 inches apart on cookie sheet.

Bake at 375° for 6 to 8 minutes. Let stand 1 minute before removing.

Orange Glazed Cranberry Christmas Cookies

This cookie comes from my aunt's kitchen and is one of my favorites. The dried bits of cranberry with the zip of orange make it practically sing on the taste buds.

  1 cup softened butter
  ½ cup sugar
  1 cup powdered sugar
  1 egg
  2 tsp. vanilla
  2¼ cup flour
  ½ tsp. baking soda
  1 cup dried cranberries
  ½ cup mini semi-sweet chocolate chips
  ½ tsp. zest of fresh orange peel

Glaze

  1 cup powdered sugar
  1 T. melted butter
  2 T. orange juice
  ¼ tsp. zest of fresh orange peel

In a large bowl, cream together butter, sugars, egg, and vanilla; beat until light and fluffy. Add in flour and baking soda and stir until combined. Mix in cranberries, chocolate chips, and zest of orange peel. Shape cookie dough into a 12-inch log, cover, and place in refrigerator until firm, at least 2 hours, or up to a couple of days. You may also freeze this dough ahead of time.

When ready to bake, preheat oven to 350°. Using a sharp knife, slice cookies to approximately ⅓-inch thick. Place on an ungreased cookie sheet and bake for 10 to 12 minutes, until cookies are set but not turning brown.

For the glaze: In a medium bowl, mix together powdered sugar, melted butter, orange juice, and zest of fresh orange peel. Pour glaze over cookies and allow to cool.

Variations: You can also substitute currants or dried blueberries in place of the cranberries.

Raisin Cookies

This cookie was first introduced to my family by a neighbor. We'd never had anything like them, and they quickly became a favorite.

During the pioneer days and the Great Depression, fruit was often dried as it could be easily carried and did not require the cost of canning, refrigerating, or the freezing. If possible, some would be saved especially for Christmas baking. With the raisins and the spices, these are a delicious cookie, served during the holidays and all year.

1 cup water
2 cups raisins
1 cup butter
2 eggs
1 tsp. vanilla
1¾ cups sugar
3½ cups flour
1 tsp. baking powder
1 tsp. baking soda
1 tsp. salt
½ tsp. cinnamon
¼ tsp. nutmeg
1 tsp. ginger
½ cup finely chopped pecans (we don't want large chunks)

Preheat oven to 350°. Combine water and raisins in a medium saucepan and bring to a boil. Simmer for 4 minutes and then let cool.

In a large mixing bowl, cream together the butter, eggs, and vanilla.

In a separate bowl, stir together the dry ingredients. Stir the dry ingredients into the large bowl with the creamed ingredients and blend well.

Add the raisins (do not drain) and the pecans to the cookie dough. Stir until combined.

Drop cookies by tablespoonful onto an ungreased cookie sheet about 2 inches apart. Bake in preheated oven for 12 to 15 minutes, until cookies are set in the middle.

Allow to cool and enjoy!

Great-Great-Grandma's Sugar Cookies

> 3 cups sifted flour
> 1 tsp. baking powder
> 1 cup butter
> 1 cup sugar
> ½ tsp. salt
> 1 egg, beaten
> 1 tsp. vanilla
> 2 T. cream

Mix 2½ cups flour and baking powder together. Cream the butter, add in sugar and salt, and then the egg, mixing until light and fluffy. (A stand mixer does this on high in a few minutes.) Mix in the vanilla and cream. Slowly add in the remaining ½ cup flour to make the dough stiff enough to roll out.

Cover dough and chill for 2 hours. This will keep for up to 3 days in the fridge, or you can pop it in the freezer for several weeks.

When ready to bake, preheat oven to 375°. On a lightly floured surface, roll the dough ⅛-inch thick. Cut into desired shapes with cookie cutters. Place onto a greased cookie sheet and bake for 12 minutes. Remove and allow to cool thoroughly.

Homemade Hot Cider with Mulling Spices

Is there anything better than hot apple cider when there's a chill in the air? I'm having a hard time coming up with anything either. Skip purchasing those bags or bottles in the store and make your own mulling spices.

> 2 4-inch cinnamon sticks
> ½ tsp. whole cloves
> 1 tsp. ginger root, grated works well
> 1 tsp. dried orange peel/zest
> 1 tsp. dried lemon peel/zest
> ½ gallon organic apple juice

If you have a large tea infusion ball, you can use that for the spices, minus the cinnamon sticks. Just put the cinnamon sticks whole in your pot.

If you don't have a large infusion ball, you can create a sachet with a piece of cheesecloth. Simply trim a piece large enough to hold the spices and tie it closed with some kitchen twine or thread.

Bring apple juice to a simmer over medium heat. Add mulling spices and allow to steep for up to 20 minutes. Remove spices and serve hot.

Hot Cocoa

> ⅓ cup cocoa powder
> ¼ cup sugar (more or less, to taste)
> 1½ cups water
> Pinch of salt
> 3 cups milk
> 1 cup cream
> ½ tsp. vanilla extract

In a medium saucepan combine cocoa powder, sugar, water, and salt over medium-low heat. Stir until smooth and then bring to a simmer. Add in the milk, cream, and vanilla and cook until hot but not boiling.

For a truly wonderful cup, use an immersion blender or hand beater and beat until frothy. Serve hot and enjoy.

Variations:

- You can use all milk or all cream, depending upon how decadent you feel for the day.

- Sprinkle with cinnamon for a little bit of spice.

- Use peppermint extract to taste.

I hope your home and holidays will be filled with love, handmade items, and traditions that will be passed down for generations to come.

* * *

I'm honored to have shared this time with you and I hope it doesn't end just because we've reached the last pages of this book.

I'd love to invite you to video tutorials, more handmade goodness, and old-fashioned wisdom from the Great Depression era in the bonus sections at www.handmadethebook.com.

Recipe Index

Barbecue Sauce 75
Bread
    Cheese 47
    Cinnamon Raisin 46
    Cinnamon Rolls 48
    French. 38
    Master Bread Dough. 43
    Pizza Dough 51
    Pizza Dough, No-Rise. 51
    Pretzels, Soft 49
    Rustic Round Loaf 45
    Regular Bread Pan Loaf. 46
    White, Old-Fashioned 40
    White, Sourdough. 103
    Sandwich, Sourdough. 104
Bread Crumbs 73
Bread Pudding
    Custard. 33
    Chocolate Custard 34
    Pumpkin Custard 35
Buttermilk
    Biscuits, Flaky. 20
    Pancakes, Overnight 117
    Pie. 24

Syrup 28

Cake
Birthday 197
Carrot with Buttermilk Syrup. 27
Chocolate Depression-Era Crazy Cake 200
Peach Pudding Cake 30
Pumpkin Applesauce Cake 29
Pumpkin Roll 207

Carrots, Roasted. 203

Chicken
30-Minute Chicken and Dumplings. 77
Chicken and Biscuit Bake .77
Chicken Dumplings 75

Chili
Chili 65
White Turkey 211

Cocoa, Hot. 245

Cookies
Chocolate Chip 19
Great-Great-Grandma's Sugar. 244
Molasses Sugar 240
Orange-Glazed Cranberry Christmas 242
Pumpkin Sugar. 205
Raisin 243

Crackers 22

Doughnuts. 35

Dumplings
Berry. 79
Chicken Dumplings 75
30-Minute Chicken and Dumplings. 77

Frosting, Buttercream. 199

Fry Bread
    Cornmeal 67
    Dessert 67
    Flour 66

Granola 115

Gravy
    Chocolate 196
    Turkey 203

Kefir 119

Mayonnaise 124

Meatballs 72

Meringue 26

Oatmeal
    Pancakes 118
    Yogurt Bowl 114
    Old-Fashioned 80

Pancakes
    Buttermilk, Overnight 117
    Sourdough 97

Pesto 151

Pizza Dough 51

Pizza Dough (No Rise) 51

Pizza Sauce (red) 53

Pizza
    Dutch Oven 85
    Fake-It Sausage 54
    Tomato Basil Chicken 52
    White Sauce Chicken 53

Pickles, Garlic Dill 106

Pie Crust
    Flaky 23
    Sourdough 99

Pie, Chocolate Meringue 25
Pumpkin Puree. 204
Pudding, Rice. 32
Sauerkraut 110
Seasoning Mixes
    Chili 149
    Italian 149
    Popcorn 150
    Ranch Dressing. 150
    Taco 148
Shepherd's Pie. 78
Smoothie 114
Soups and Stews
    Chicken Stock. 64
    Crab Bisque 70
    Ham and Broccoli Chowder .68
    Son of a Gun Stew 69
Sour cream 122
Sourdough
    Pancakes 97
    Pie Crust. 99
    Starter. 94
    Torillas 98
    Waffles 97
    White Bread 103
    Whole Wheat Sandwich Bread 104
Spaghetti and Meatballs 71
Sugar, Powdered 38
Turkey
    Roasted. 202
    Turkey Skillet Supper 210
Yogurt. 112

Herbal Remedies

Bath Salts **166**

Decoctions **154**

Infused Oil **158**

Lip Balm **160**

Salves or Balms **161**

Tea Infusions **154**

Tinctures **155**

Homespun Crafts, Gifts, Decor

Beeswax Candles **214**

Canning Lid Christmas Ornaments **233**

Christmas Fudge **235**

Christmas Potpourri **234**

Cinnamon Salt Dough Ornaments **231**

Hot Cider with Mulling Spices **245**

Melt-and-Pour Lemon Lime Soap **221**

Oatmeal Honey Soap (cold process method) **226**

Peppermint Chocolate Body Lotion **163**

Skin-Soothing Salve **162**

Notes

Chapter 1: Bake

1. Trust me. I've tried doing it by hand, and it never formed stiff peaks and the next day my arm would barely work.

Chapter 3: Culture

1. Heather B. Patisaul and Wendy Jefferson, "The Pros and Cons of Phytoestrogens," National Center for Biotechnology Information, March 27, 2010, doi: 10.1016/j.yfrne.2010.03.003, https://www.ncbi.nlm.nih.gov/pmc/articles/PMC3074428/

Chapter 4: Thrive

1. University of Maryland Medical Center, Complementary and Alternative Medicine Guide, Herb, "Arnica": http://umm.edu/health/medical/altmed/herb/arnica

2. Janmejai K Srivastava, Eswar Shankar, and Sanjay Gupta, "Chamomile," https://www.ncbi.nlm.nih.gov/pmc/articles/PMC2995283/

3. "Coumarin," https://en.wikipedia.org/wiki/Coumarin

4. WebMD, Vitamins and Supplements, "Comfrey," http://www.webmd.com/vitamins-supplements/ingredientmono-295-comfrey.aspx?activeingredientid=295&activeingredientname=comfrey

5. S. Hosseinzadeh, M.J. Ghalesefidi, M.Azami, M.A. Mohaghegh, S.H. Hejazi, M. Ghomashlooyan, "In Vitro and In Vivo Anthelmintic Activity of Seed Extract of Coriandrum Sativum Compared to Niclosamid Against Hymenolepis Nana Infection," https://www.ncbi.nlm.nih.gov/pubmed/27876936

6. P.S. Chauhan, N.K. Satti, K.A. Suri, M.Amina, S. Bani, "Stimulatory Effects of Cuminum Cyminum and Flavonoid Glycoside on Cyclosporine-A and Restraint Stress Induced Immune-Suppression in Swiss Albino Mice," https://www.ncbi.nlm.nih.gov/pubmed/20156427

7. University of Maryland Medical Center, Complementary and Alternative Medicine Guide, Herb, "Dandelion," http://umm.edu/health/medical/altmed/herb/dandelion

8. WebMD, Vitamins and Supplements, "Garlic," http://www.webmd.com/vitamins-supplements/ingredientmono-300-garlic.aspx?activeingredientid=300

9. WebMD, Vitamins and Supplements, "Ginger," http://www.webmd.com/vitamins-supplements/ingredientmono-961-ginger.aspx?activeingredientid=961

10. T. Al-Howiriny, A. Alsheikh, S. Alqasoumi, M. Al-Yahya, K. ElTahir, S. Rafatullah, "Protective

Effect of Origanum Majorana L. 'Marjoram' on "Various Models of Gastric Mucosal Injury in Rats," https://www.ncbi.nlm.nih.gov/pubmed/19606513

11. I. Haj-Husein, S. Tukan, F. Alkazaleh, "The Effect of Marjoram (Origanum Majorana) Tea on the Hormonal Profile of Women with Polycystic Ovary Syndrome," https://www.ncbi.nlm.nih.gov/pubmed/25662759

12. "Marshmallow," http://www.webmd.com/vitamins-supplements/ingredientmono-774-marshmallow.aspx?activeIngredientId=774&activeIngredientName=marshmallow

13. H. Yuan, M. Zhu, W. Guo, L. Jin, W. Chen, U.T. Brunk, M. Zhao, "Mustard Seeds (Sinapis Alba Linn) Attenuate Azoxymethane-Induced Colon Carcinogenesis," https://www.ncbi.nlm.nih.gov/pubmed/21605497

14. WebMD, Vitamins and Supplements, "Nutmeg and Mace," http://www.webmd.com/vitamins-supplements/ingredientmono-788-nutmeg%20and%20mace.aspx?activeingredientid=788&activeingredientname=nutmeg%20and%20mace

15. WebMD, Vitamins and Supplements, "Great Plantain," http://www.webmd.com/vitamins-supplements/ingredientmono-677-great%20plantain.aspx?activeingredientid=677&activeingredientname=great%20plantain

16. WebMD, Vitamins and Supplements, "Sage," http://www.webmd.com/vitamins-supplements/ingredientmono-504-SAGE.aspx?activeIngredientId=504&activeIngredientName=SAGE&source=2

17. WebMD, Vitamins and Supplements, "Stinging Nettle," http://www.webmd.com/vitamins-supplements/ingredientmono-664-stinging%20nettle.aspx?activeingredientid=664

18. Michael Greger M.D. FACLM, "Why Pepper Boosts Turmeric Blood Levels," http://nutritionfacts.org/2015/02/05/why-pepper-boosts-turmeric-blood-levels/

19. Behnood Abbasi, Masud Kimiagar, Khosro Sadeghniiat, Minoo M. Shirazi, Mehdi Hedayati, and Bahram Rashidkhan, "The Effect of Magnesium Supplementation on Primary Insomnia in Elderly," https://www.ncbi.nlm.nih.gov/pmc/articles/PMC3703169/

20. A. Serefko, A. Szopa, E. Poleszak, "Magnesium and depression," https://www.ncbi.nlm.nih.gov/pubmed/27910808

21. Tara Parker-Pope, "The Science of Chicken Soup," Well Blog, *The New York Times,* October 12, 2007, https://well.blogs.nytimes.com/2007/10/12/the-science-of-chicken-soup/

The Made from Scratch Life

Do you long for simpler days? Do you wish you had the time to offer your family home-grown meals? Does your heart cry for a quiet place in this fast-paced world?

In *The Made-from-Scratch Life*, blogger and homesteader Melissa K. Norris inspires with more practical and easy methods to help you garden and preserve your own food, and see God's fingerprints in your everyday busy life. You'll learn how to

- plan, plant, and harvest for eating and preserving
- troubleshoot common gardening problems with natural solutions
- improve your family's health with natural cooking and cleaning methods

Whether you live in the middle of the asphalt jungle or on the side of a mountain, you can experience the pioneer lifestyle and start your own homesteading journey. Because when you surround yourself with things made from the hand of God, you can't help but see Him.

About the Author

Melissa K. Norris shares old-fashioned wisdom and skills for a modern world with her books, podcasts, and blog. Melissa lives with her husband and two children in their own little house in the big woods in the foothills of the North Cascade Mountains. When she's not wrangling chickens and cattle, you can find her stuffing Mason jars with homegrown food and playing with flour and sugar in the kitchen.

To learn more about
Melissa K. Norris or this book, go to
www.melissaknorris.com
www.handmadethebook.com
or to read sample chapters, visit our website at
www.harvesthousepublishers.com